Historic
North American
Locomotives
An Illustrated Journey

KEN BOYD

Kalmbach
Media

DEDICATION

This book is dedicated with love to my parents,
Wesley and Lula Mae Boyd.

Kalmbach Media
21027 Crossroads Circle
Waukesha, Wisconsin 53186
www.KalmbachHobbyStore.com

Published in 2018

22 21 20 19 18   1 2 3 4 5

Manufactured in China

ISBN: 978-1-62700-508-1
EISBN: 978-1-62700-509-8

Editors: Randy Rehberg, Jeff Wilson
Book Design: Tom Ford

Library of Congress Control Number: 2017941415

Transition from steam to electric and diesel

Final advances in steam development

Postwar technologies

Modern era

INTRODUCTION

The locomotive has always been much more than a method of transport. For more than 200 years, painters, photographers, writers, and musicians have shared their visions commemorating the power and magnificence of the locomotive. Locomotive builders and designers have long shown their passion for these massive machines by producing not only functional engines but ones that make statements on energy, form, and style. As a result, locomotives endure as inspirational marvels of technology. Today, the locomotive remains as captivating and entrancing as it was in the early days of the 1800s.

As a young adult, I became fascinated with both locomotives and photography. That was almost four decades ago. Just as locomotive designs evolved over time, my understanding of light and appreciation for composition progressed, along with my artistic vision and photographic skills—first with film in the wet darkroom and later with the digital camera and the computer. I always wanted to learn and improve. As was Ansel Adams' objective, my goal as a photographer is not to just *take* pictures but to *make* fine-art images.

When I see a locomotive on location, I attempt to visualize how my final image will look. Where are the potential problem areas? What is needed to improve the image? Are additional shots of details or ones from other angles necessary? Do I have everything I need when I get to my computer to make the image I have visualized? Ultimately, my goal is to make a passionate and definitive statement about these locomotives—to present them with enhanced detail and vibrant colors, and to provide an uplifting and artistically idealized representation of each locomotive.

As a follow-up to my earlier book *The Art of the Locomotive*, I began to consider the possibility of producing an entire book with all of the primary locomotive images presented on a clean, simple, and uncluttered background. Background removal is an elegant approach for many photographic images, especially those with detailed and mechanical subjects like locomotives that are often set against cluttered backgrounds. For this book, I extracted more than 200 historic locomotive images from their backgrounds, leaving the locomotives as portraits on rails or roadbeds. This was a tedious but rewarding process.

My overall process involved much more than presenting the locomotives on clean backgrounds. While every attempt was made to take each photograph in the best possible light, locomotives can be challenging to photograph since they are reflective subjects and often characterized by dark shadows and bright shiny highlights. I have spent many hours retouching and detailing the images presented in this book to reveal the intricacy, uniqueness, and charm of each locomotive. Every bolt, linkage, and cable has been revisited and refined to assure that readers are provided with the best possible image of each locomotive.

Throughout the book, ancillary images accompany the primary images to provide insight and perspective that might be lost without the framework and context of a background. Some of these images also provide scenes with locomotives in operation and on location as a complement to the primary portraits. In

MY OBJECTIVE, MY GOAL AS

A PHOTOGRAPHER IS NOT

TO JUST TAKE PICTURES BUT

TO MAKE FINE-ART IMAGES.

addition, I have included a few images of European locomotives to illustrate important connections to engineering developments across the Atlantic as American technology evolved.

Along with the photographic images, you will find basic information about each locomotive, such as dates of construction or rebuild and alternative names and numbers that were used over the years. I have also offered selective yet relevant commentary and observations about the locomotives, their operations, and the railroads. This book emphasizes the beautiful and amazing locomotives from the 1800s, but I have also included a sampling of 20th century locomotives.

Some images in the book were taken at the world's greatest transportation museums and these are credited. Other images are photographs taken at outdoor locations across the North American continent. Both original and historic-replica locomotives have been included to more completely convey the story of this remarkable machine.

Join me, as we reflect on the wonderful and remarkable visual history of the North American locomotive!

A depot's directional weather vane

HISTORICAL PERSPECTIVE

Beginning in the early 1800s, the locomotive led America and the world through the Industrial Revolution, one of the most significant social and economic transformations in history. The locomotive transported people and materials, connected vast expanses of continents, and enriched lives with a new reality never before imagined. Travel that had previously taken weeks or months, if even possible, could now be achieved in hours or days.

The steam locomotive progressed with each iteration and refinement in concept and design to become more formidable, capable, and splendid. As materials, technologies, and construction techniques evolved during the Industrial Revolution, so did the locomotive. Steel, which was stronger and lighter, replaced the iron materials of earlier locomotives. Boiler pressures increased and efficiencies improved. Mechanical linkages and steam cycles were refined and optimized.

At the same time, rail and track materials and structural and civil engineering techniques advanced to address daunting bridge, trestle, and tunnel construction projects. Roadbeds were reinforced as locomotives grew larger and faster to accommodate increasingly greater loads and growing demands. Signaling and safety became paramount considerations and evolved to exacting and precise sciences.

The 19th century was an era of great experimentation in locomotive design, and while some concepts succeeded, others failed. Ideas flowed across America and to Europe and back, and designers built on the successes of earlier machines to meet specific needs by region and railroad. Wheel diameters and arrangements, boiler proportions and chimney styles, cylinder and drive linkage assemblies, and other engineering and cosmetic parameters varied greatly.

Designs became highly stylized, and by the 1840s, locomotives developed into grand machines with Victorian appointments featuring elaborate and colorful paint schemes. Brass and copper details shimmered brightly and were fitted wherever possible on bells, whistles, headlamps, sand domes, cowcatchers, and trim. Pinstripes lined the wheels, the boiler, and the cab. Rich and lustrously polished woodwork and luminous Russian iron were added to cover hot surfaces that could not sustain the early paints. These 19th century locomotives were among the most beautiful machines ever produced. The designers and sometimes the general public gave these locomotives fanciful names to match their often elaborate and varied trappings—names like *Rocket, Tom Thumb, Grasshopper, American, Monster, Highwheel, Crampton, Fairlie, Camelback, Mogul, Mikado, Prairie*, and *Big Boy*.

Thousands of locomotives were built in larger railroad machine shops, by numerous small manufacturers, and at several massive production facilities. Reliability, safety and cost became more and more important over time and designs gradually standardized. As this standardization continued into the late 1800s, some of the smaller shops closed or merged, and only a few very large manufacturers and some major railroads continued to produce locomotives. These companies concentrated primarily on designing enormous locomotives to be used mainly for hauling heavy cargo over long distances.

By the 1880s, most manufacturers and railroads had switched the fuel source of steam locomotives from wood to coal because coal contained more energy and the supply seemed unlimited. This change to coal did not appeal to the locomotive crews or to the towns and people along the tracks since it was dirtier and more difficult to handle than wood. Over

time, the locomotives, railcars, and everything along the tracks became coated with a black coal residue. The switch to coal was also responsible for American locomotives losing much of their splendor. The colorful Victorian styling on locomotives began to disappear as they took on a more utilitarian function. They were often painted black to better hide the coal residue on the engines. During the austerity of World War I and World War II, black became an almost universal color for locomotives. Still, some decorated and colorful locomotives were maintained, especially for use on passenger trains, and happily some survive to this day.

Many other significant advances in locomotive development occurred in the late 19th century and early 20th century. Boilers and fireboxes were enlarged. Compounding of steam engines allowed designers to add third and fourth cylinders and linkages to use steam twice (reuse exhaust steam) and increase power and efficiency. Superheating steam at higher pressures reduced fuel and water consumption and released a tremendous amount of additional energy. Articulation allowed longer locomotives to flex around tight turns in the tracks. Wheel configurations progressed from relatively simple 0-4-0, 4-4-0, and 4-6-2 designs to remarkable compounded, superheated, and articulated arrangements as elaborate as 4-12-2, 4-8-8-4, and 2-10-10-2.

In the years following World War I, steam locomotives became ever larger, heavier, faster, and

The 1898 Mobile & Ohio wooden and steel trestle crosses the Black Warrior River in Alabama. Railway engineering as exemplified by this 3,600-foot structure transformed the American landscape.

more powerful for express passenger and freight services. During this era, steam locomotive design and technology achieved its pinnacle of refinement. By the 1940s, the finest steam locomotives ever built were operating across North America, Europe, and other regions of the world. But the end of World War II marked the close of the steam locomotive era.

The new rail-related technologies that began to emerge at the turn of the 20th century would eventually transform the locomotive from the classic steam engine to more modern forms of traction. As the 20th century progressed, railroads adopted electric, diesel, diesel-electric, and a few turbine locomotives. These new tractive methods helped reduce maintenance, lessen air pollution, enhance safety, improve performance, and lower costs. By the 1960s, the transformation away from steam, which had been delayed by World War II, was complete in most areas of America.

But even as locomotive technologies evolved, other means of transportation improved also. The public readily embraced these alternatives to locomotives. By mid-century, new roads and highway systems were being built across the country. Newer and fancier car models appealed to the public, and overland hauling companies were using more efficient trucks. Travelers preferred the convenience and privacy of the automobile, especially on long-distance trips, and trucks offered a competitive alternative to trains for freight transport. The airplane became a faster way to carry people and transport cargo across great distances. Faced with these alternatives to rail transportation, ever-tightening governmental regulations, and a host of other pressures, railroads entered an era of decline.

Many ceased operations, while others merged or became state railroads, and the era of the locomotive seemed to have ended, at least for a time.

Given the fierce freight truck competition in the 1980s and 1990s, the remaining railroads refocused their purpose. Regulation of railroad operations was relaxed somewhat. As trade and markets continued to become more international, railroads captured the new containerized, modal freight shipment sector by moving products as diverse as books, electronics, automobiles, clothing, and food from ports and factories to distributors, retailers, and consumers. Passenger traffic increased again as automobiles and trucks experienced gridlocked roadway congestion, higher fuel and initial purchase costs, and safety and environmental concerns.

In the late 20th century, faster and more modern locomotives and expanded rail networks reestablished train travel as a valid option for commuting and long-distance journeys. By this time, sleek, high-speed locomotives had arrived. These locomotives running at speeds approaching, and sometimes exceeding, 200 miles per hour allowed the railroads to compete with air travel in some markets.

The millennium has brought with it a new generation of locomotive enthusiasts. These new admirers value and validate the old historic technologies and appreciate the new designs. Steam and early diesel and electric locomotives have been restored, either cosmetically or to full operational condition. Today, there is a new awareness and appreciation for historical preservation.

This book is intended to enhance the 21st century enthusiasm for historic locomotives and our enduring and evolving railroading history.

Kansas City Southern No. 691 with an approaching storm

Southern Railway No. 4501 under steam and waiting at an ancient platform

EARLY LOCOMOTIVES

The first steam locomotives were designed and demonstrated in Britain during the early 1800s. The first American-made locomotive was tested in 1825 on the estate of Colonel John Stevens. Through the 1830s, a number of locomotives were imported by the United States and Canada from Britain, and other locomotives were built domestically in shops along the east coast of the United States. These early locomotives were primitive contraptions, but they clearly demonstrated the potential and capabilities of this new technology.

During the 1840s, numerous locomotive and railway designs and concepts were evaluated and tested to best meet the needs for North American passengers and freight. By this time, a number of locomotive builders were emerging in the United States.

Steam Waggon, 1825
(John Stevens Locomotive)

I n the United States, John Stevens is generally considered to be the "Father of the American Railroad," a deserving tribute. Stevens was a man of vision, and he was especially interested in transportation technologies. In the early 1800s, he faced powerful canal-operator opposition and financial constraints to his ideas for various railroading projects. In 1825, when he was 75 years old, he decided to design, finance, and build a demonstration locomotive and circular railroad track on his estate in Hoboken, New Jersey. It was this project and his *Steam Waggon* that introduced North America to the steam locomotive and railroading design.

Through 1826 and 1827, he operated his locomotive, which was basically a wooden wagon with a small steam engine and a cog-and-rack drive system. The machine could attain speeds of up to 12 miles per hour with several passengers onboard. It ran on wheels without typical flanges, but instead used some sort of retainers to avoid derailment. For demonstrations at his estate, passengers rode on the actual *Steam Waggon* with Stevens and the boiler and not in trailing passenger coaches.

A 1928 replica of the locomotive is on display at the Museum of Science and Industry in Chicago. A second 1939 replica is preserved at the Railroad Museum of Pennsylvania. These replicas are based in part on the recollection of Stevens' grandson who witnessed the *Steam Waggon* in operation.

This *Steam Waggon* replica is displayed at the Railroad Museum of Pennsylvania.

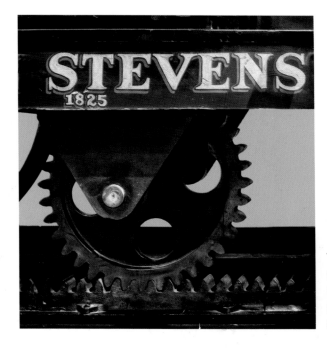

The wooden cog-and-rack drive system is shown on the *Steam Waggon* at the Museum of Science and Industry in Chicago.

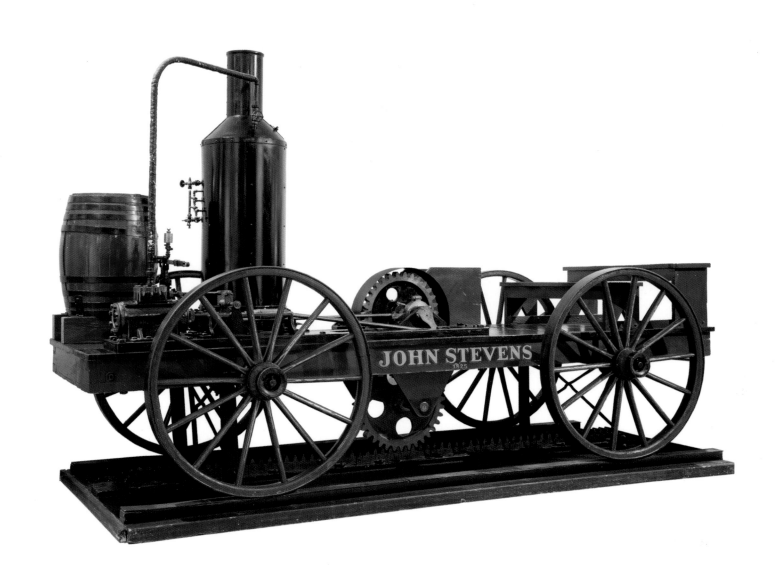

ROCKET, 1829

In 1829, the Liverpool & Manchester Railway held a locomotive competition, known as the Rainhill Trials, to evaluate the state of the technology. Five designs were tested. The winner was the *Rocket* by George Stephenson. Coming in second was the *Sans Pareil* by Timothy Hackworth, which also proved to be a successful design. In the 1830s, the technology of the *Rocket* and the *Sans Pareil* came to America and spread to developed areas across western Europe.

Today, the Stephenson *Rocket* is probably the world's most famous locomotive and has been the inspiration for numerous model trains and toys, games, and puzzles; mechanical engineering exercises; artwork, displays, and medallions; and a number of replicas.

Because of its popularity and highly practical, efficient, and reliable design elements, the locomotive was copied around the world for many years. The *Rocket*'s wheel arrangement is now known as 0-2-2, and the locomotive was designed as a 4-foot, 8½-inch "Stephenson" gauge machine, a track spacing now known as standard gauge.

At least nine high-quality replicas have been built since 1881. The first working replica was commissioned by Henry Ford and built in 1929 by Robert Stephenson & Company at their locomotive works in Darlington, United Kingdom. The replica was created from the original drawings, illustrations, and written accounts of George Stephenson.

This locomotive is exhibited today at the Henry Ford Museum in Dearborn, Michigan. A second replica was built by Robert Stephenson & Company in 1931 and is currently on display at the Museum of Science and Industry in Chicago, Illinois. Two additional replicas of the *Rocket* can be seen at the National Railway Museum in York, United Kingdom.

Both the original *Rocket* (left) and the *Sans Pareil* (right) are now preserved in museums in London and Shildon, United Kingdom, respectively.

TOM THUMB, 1830

(COOPER LOCOMOTIVE)

This little locomotive is the subject of one of the most memorable American children's stories. It was also a landmark in technological and transportation history. To build the *Tom Thumb*, a talented businessman and engineer, Peter Cooper, acquired a small, roughly 1.4-horsepower steam engine and fitted it to a two-axle cart with a vertical boiler and a vertical cylinder linked to one of the two axles. This wheel arrangement was later identified as a 2-2-0. The engine was fired with anthracite coal. Cooper named his locomotive *Tom Thumb* because he considered it to be so small and unworthy.

As the story goes, *Tom Thumb* pulled a railcar with about 20 Baltimore & Ohio directors and other officials on a demonstration from Baltimore to Ellicott Mills, a distance of about 13 miles. The locomotive's performance was impressive, and the trip out went fine. On the way back, where the track became a double line into Baltimore, a horse cart challenged *Tom Thumb* to a race, in what was actually a rigged event with a very fast horse. Regardless, the locomotive was winning the race until the blower belt slipped off and became entangled. The locomotive lost power. The horse went on to win the race, but the railroad officials were impressed by the demonstration and realized that steam locomotive technology was needed to build their railroad and compete with the canal companies of that era.

Baltimore & Ohio built a replica of the original *Tom Thumb* in 1927 for the railroad's Fair of the Iron Horse. It is now displayed at the Baltimore & Ohio Railroad Museum. Although this replica was carefully designed, it is thought to vary considerably from the original locomotive.

Tom Thumb's blower belt

BEST FRIEND OF CHARLESTON, 1830

In December 1830, the *Best Friend of Charleston* became the first locomotive manufactured entirely in the United States for commercial service. It was designed by Horatio Allen and built by the West Point Foundry in New York. The *Best Friend* was an 0-4-0, 5-foot gauge, wood-fired engine with a tall vertical boiler and rod-connected drivers. It carried water in a reservoir built into the base of the engine, which provided good traction for pulling.

The *Best Friend* began operation on Christmas Day in 1830 by pulling several cars and a total of 141 passengers over a 6-mile line "annihilating time and space on the wings of wind at 15 to 25 miles per hour" (according to the *Charleston Courier* newspaper).

The locomotive was then placed into regular passenger service until it suffered a deadly boiler explosion in 1831. The boiler exploded after an untrained and ill-fated fireman either wired the pressure relief valve shut or sat on a board that blocked the safety valve operation.

Following the explosion, the parts were reassembled and the locomotive was named *Phoenix* because it rose from the ashes. To calm the concerns of passengers about another possible explosion, a car loaded with six bales of cotton was placed behind the tender and in front of the first passenger car to serve as a shield from scalding water and flying debris.

Two full-size replicas exist. The pictured replica is housed in a museum gallery in Charleston, and a second replica can be seen at the South Carolina State Museum in Columbia.

The Best Friend of Charleston is shown here in classic Southern Railway colors.

DeWitt Clinton, 1831

In 1831, West Point Foundry in New York was continuing to learn about and build locomotives. Along with the *Best Friend of Charleston*, one of its most famous engines, the *DeWitt Clinton*, was built for the Mohawk & Hudson Railroad in New York. The intent was to develop a design for a locomotive that could pull a heavier load than the 0-2-0 British engines that were being imported.

The *DeWitt Clinton* was a beautiful locomotive, but it was plagued by fundamental design flaws from the beginning. The chimney was too large for proper drafting, and the water from the boiler flowed into the cylinders. Even after these problems were corrected, the ride was rough and lurching. The locomotive did offer a cover for the tender that somewhat protected the crew from the elements, all-iron wheels instead of partial wood ones, and a water tank built into the tender to be used along with barrels of water carried on board. Inside cylinders made for a very clean look.

Much to the pleasure of political and financial competition from the Erie Canal owners and operators, freight wagon companies, inn keepers and toll road proprietors, the inaugural run of the *Clinton* did not go well. The engine and set of cars managed to operate for about a year before they were retired.

A beautiful replica of this locomotive is on exhibit today in the Henry Ford Museum in Dearborn, Michigan.

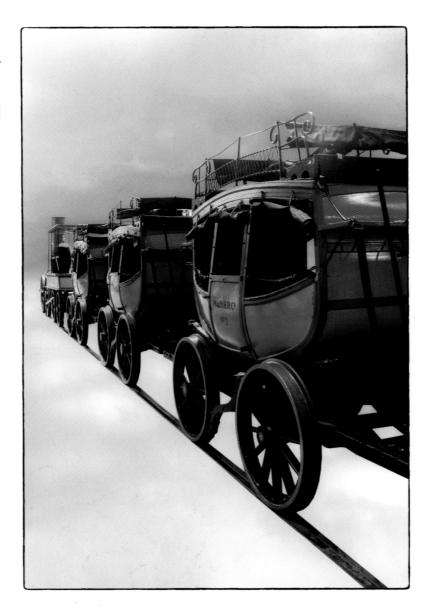

DeWitt Clinton replica coaches at the Henry Ford Museum

YORK, 1831

(DAVIS LOCOMOTIVE)

A ride on the *Tom Thumb*, even if it did lose a race against a horse, was enough to convince the executives and directors at the Baltimore & Ohio Railroad that steam-powered locomotives could be just the ticket for competing with the canal companies. So in 1831, the railroad announced a competition, open to all, for the best locomotive design. Five, or by some accounts six, entries responded and the entry by Phineas Davis of York, Pennsylvania, was judged the winner.

His locomotive was named *York*. Apparently, *York* was not only the best locomotive but the only satisfactory entry—that is, it actually operated. The York was an 0-4-0, 3½-ton engine with a vertical boiler and two cylinders. It was built to fire anthracite coal, which was common at that time. The locomotive's wheelbase was very short and the drivers were 30 inches in diameter. Davis was awarded chief locomotive engineer status with the B&O, where he ultimately built 20 locomotives based on the *York*'s design.

The original *York* may no longer be with us, but a replica was built at the Baltimore & Ohio Mt. Claire Shops for the railroad's Fair of the Iron Horse in 1927. The replica was also exhibited at the 1933–1934 Chicago World's Fair and was displayed for many years in beautiful condition at the Museum of Science and Industry in Chicago. Today, the locomotive is on exhibit at the Baltimore & Ohio Railroad Museum.

York and tender

JOHN BULL, 1831

The *John Bull* exhibit at the Smithsonian Institute in Washington, D.C., is one of the most striking and noteworthy railroading exhibits in the world. This authentic, classically beautiful, woodburning Camden & Amboy 4-2-0 locomotive is one of the foremost historical and technological treasures of the United States. It was built in Newcastle, England, by George and Robert Stephenson & Company, disassembled, shipped across the Atlantic, and reassembled.

Isaac Dripps, a young American mechanic, assembled the engine without drawings and having never seen a locomotive! He added a cart to function as the tender and outfitted it with a whiskey barrel for water and a leather tube or pipe to supply the water to the boiler.

The *John Bull* originally had an 0-4-0 wheel arrangement with a horizontal boiler and a vertical chimney. Because of problems with derailments and obstacles along the track, Dripps added a leading truck and cowcatcher to guide the locomotive through turns and clear the track of obstacles— a noteworthy industry first. With these modifications, the wheel arrangement became 4-2-0, leaving only one set of powered driving wheels. In addition, an enclosed cab, bell, and headlight were added later. The official name of the locomotive was *Stevens*, or No. 1, but the crews referred to it as *Old John Bull* from an English cartoon and the name stuck.

In 1833, the *John Bull* derailed and killed two passengers, the first passenger deaths recorded in the United States by a locomotive. The locomotive operated in service for about 35 years.

Agenoria, 1829

Most early American locomotives, such as the *John Bull, Dorchester,* and *Stourbridge Lion* came from Britain. The *Stourbridge Lion* was the first locomotive to operate commercially in America, although very briefly, and today only the boiler survives at the Smithsonian Institute. *Agenoria* is believed to be essentially identical to the *Stourbridge Lion,* and it is preserved at the National Railway Museum in York, United Kingdom. In addition, a replica locomotive has been built and can be viewed in Honesdale, Pennsylvania.

PENNSYLVANIA RAILROAD No. 1, 1831

Pennsylvania Railroad No. 1 is a 1939 replica of the 1831 *John Bull*. Compared with the *John Bull* on display at the Smithsonian, the replica has a taller and larger chimney, green paint, and a few other cosmetic and technical refinements. The intent at the Pennsylvania's Juanita Shops was to produce an identical locomotive down to the iron bolts and wood specifications, but with a safer, more modern boiler and firebox. This replica is sometimes referred to as *John Bull*, but it should not be confused with the original in Washington, D.C. The locomotive is on display at the Railroad Museum of Pennsylvania, along with the 1836 Camden & Amboy Coach No. 1, second-oldest passenger coach in the United States.

The replica was built by Pennsylvania Railroad as a replacement for the original *John Bull* for exhibit at the 1939–1940 New York World's Fair. After the World's Fair and other events over the next few decades, and while the railroad struggled through hard financial times, No. 1 sat for years in the weather and deteriorated; it was cosmetically restored at the Railroad Museum of Pennsylvania in 1982 and 1983 but currently is not certified for operation, given the issue of complying with more recent steam boiler safety certification regulations.

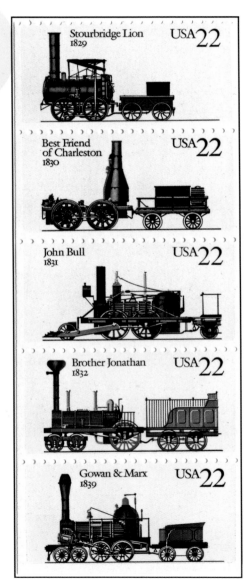

These U. S. postage stamps commemorate famous early American locomotives including *John Bull*.

ATLANTIC/ANDREW JACKSON, 1832/1836/1892

The first of 20 locomotives built for the Baltimore & Ohio Railroad was the *Atlantic* in 1832. Although the *Atlantic*, like the earlier *York*, was an 0-4-0, vertical boiler, two-cylinder, anthracite coal machine, it was said to be a much-improved model. It was heavier for better traction at 6½ tons, and the boiler and firebox were upgraded. The *Atlantic* and the 19 subsequent locomotives all performed very well, were economical, and some continued in service for more than 60 years. (These engines were popularly known as "Grasshoppers" because the cylinder design and their linkage appearance looked somewhat like a grasshopper with long angular legs.) Cabs were also added on later models. Ultimately, they were replaced by horizontal boiler locomotives when larger and more powerful designs were required. The vertical boilers on the Grasshoppers were tall and top heavy and the locomotives were built on a short wheelbase, making them somewhat unstable at high speeds.

Somehow, the *Atlantic* was mysteriously scrapped in 1835 just after the designer, Phineas Davis, was killed in a railroading accident. In 1892, the 1836 Baltimore & Ohio No. 7 *Andrew Jackson*, another Grasshopper locomotive, was modified to recreate the scrapped *Atlantic*. This locomotive was exhibited at the 1893 World Columbian Exposition in Chicago, at the 1939–1940 New York World's Fair, and at the 1948–1949 Chicago Railroad Fair. The locomotive is now on display with period stagecoach-type cars in the roundhouse at the Baltimore & Ohio Railroad Museum. By some accounts, this *Atlantic/Andrew Jackson* hybrid is the second oldest locomotive in the United States.

Now at the Baltimore & Ohio Railroad Museum, *John Hancock*, 1836, was the first Baltimore & Ohio locomotive with a cab.

MISSISSIPPI, 1834

Railroads were a little later in developing across the agricultural southeastern United States than along the mid-Atlantic coast. Areas like Mississippi were still borderline frontier in the 1820s and 1830s. Nevertheless, the *Mississippi* dates to 1834 and is believed to be the oldest surviving southern locomotive. Little can be substantiated about the locomotive, but it is thought to have been built by the English manufacturer Braithwaite and Milner (Braithwaite and Ericsson at the time). The locomotive likely came to Mississippi through New York, after being assembled in a shop somewhere there near the coast.

Mississippi initially operated on the 19-mile Natchez & Hamburg Railroad and was later used to transport cotton around the Vicksburg area. It may have seen action during the Civil War and later operated on the Vicksburg & Warrenton short line, where it apparently derailed and was abandoned.

Next, it turned up on the Meridian, Brookhaven & Natchez, which became part of the Illinois Central. From there, it made its way to Chicago for the 1893 World Columbian Exposition (Chicago World's Fair). After the exposition, the locomotive was displayed in the Chicago Palace of Fine Arts until the 1933–1934 New York World's Fair. After the fair, the *Mississippi* became an exhibit at the Museum of Science and Industry in Chicago but was sold at auction in 2015 and as of 2017 is not on public display.

The *Mississippi* is a woodburner with 43-inch drivers at a weight of about 2½ tons. The original tender was lost long ago. The locomotive is currently mated with a replica Illinois Central tender.

Mississippi, 1834, as displayed at the Chicago Museum of Science and Industry in 2015

DORCHESTER, 1836

In 1836, *Dorchester* became the first locomotive to operate in Canada. The original *Dorchester* was the 127th locomotive built by Robert Stephenson & Company in Newcastle, England. It was purchased by a group of Canadian businessmen for £1,500 and shipped to Montreal with an engineer/technician to provide setup and training. The engineer arrived with the *Dorchester*, but he immediately skipped town and left the owners without any setup or operational expertise. As a result, the engine was damaged when it ran low on water.

Once repaired, it operated satisfactorily at 20 miles per hour, although it had a high center of gravity and was described as "skittish," leading to the nickname *Iron Kitten*. Most locomotives constructed through the early 1830s were based on this four-wheel design.

In 1833, a 2-2-2 wheel arrangement was patented in Britain to improve stability and to better distribute the weight of the locomotive. An early example of this design is *Bayard*, which operated in Naples, Italy. It was capable of speeds exceeding 30 miles per hour with seven coaches in tow and fewer derailments.

In 1932, to commemorate the original *Dorchester*, a beautiful replica was constructed by volunteers at Chateau Ramezay. This replica is now on display near the entrance of Exporail, the Canadian National Railway Museum in Saint Constant, Quebec.

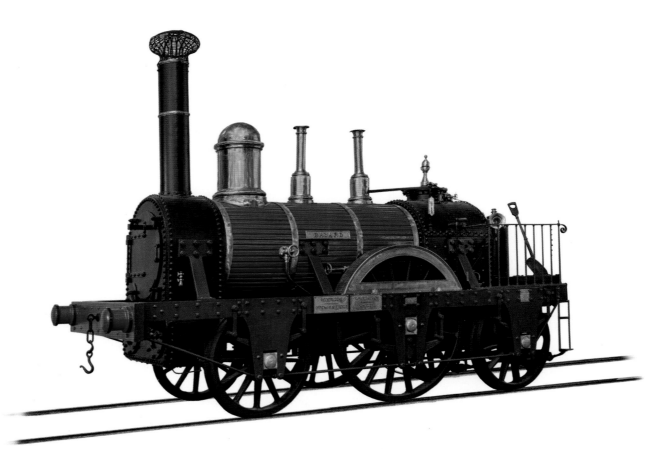

Bayard, 1839

This locomotive is representative of the 2-2-2 wheel design that demonstrated significantly improved stability and weight distribution.

RALEIGH, 1836

The *Raleigh* is a replica of the first steam locomotive to operate in North Carolina. This replica was built in 1927 by the Seaboard Air Line shops in Raleigh, North Carolina.

The original *Raleigh* was one of two 0-4-0 locomotives built in 1836 by Charles Tayleur & Company of Warrington, England, for the Raleigh & Gaston Railroad. Charles Tayleur & Company, also known as Vulcan Foundry, built locomotives through an affiliation with Robert Stephenson & Company, the premier locomotive builder in the world at that time.

Along with the second locomotive, *Gaston*, *Raleigh* was initially used in 1840 to construct an 86-mile railroad, the Raleigh & Gaston. *Raleigh* provided three decades of service, likely passenger and freight operation, as well as construction duties. During the Civil War, *Raleigh* saw action on both sides.

Raleigh & Gaston became part of the Seaboard Air Line in 1900 and eventually merged into the CSX.

The replica is exhibited very nicely indoors at the North Carolina Transportation Museum in Spencer.

Detail of *Raleigh*'s drive wheels and connection linkage

LAFAYETTE, 1837
(NORRIS LOCOMOTIVE)

In 1837, the 4-2-0 *Lafayette* was built by William and Septimus Norris in Philadelphia for the Baltimore & Ohio at what was later known as the Norris Locomotive Works, a leading steam locomotive manufacturer for several decades. The locomotive was named for the famous Revolutionary War hero, Marquis Lafayette. The design features a horizontal boiler and a four-wheel pilot/lead truck to reduce derailments.

This was the first Baltimore & Ohio locomotive with a lead truck; many more would follow. The cylinders were located outside the frame and near the smokebox at the front of the engine. The piston linkage connected directly to the drive wheels from the cylinders. Significantly, the slanted, almost horizontal cylinders were less damaging to rails than the pounding of vertical cylinders on some locomotives of the time.

The engine design was based on an economical "bar-frame" concept, which became relatively popular in Europe and hundreds were built there. The weight of the locomotive was placed as much as possible on the drivers to reduce slippage and improve tractive effort.

A 1927 replica of the *Lafayette* was built for the Fair of the Iron Horse. It is still considered operable and is on display in superb cosmetic condition at the Baltimore & Ohio Railroad Museum.

Perspective view of *Lafayette*

SAMSON, 1838

Samson is the oldest surviving locomotive in Canada and one of the oldest in North America. It was ordered in 1837 and was designed and built in 1838 by Timothy Hackworth in Shildon, England. It is one of three surviving Hackworth locomotives, with the oldest being the *Sans Pareil* from 1829.

The 0-6-0, vertical cylinder, coal-fired engine was considered to be a highly successful design and a strong puller but slow; its maximum speed was about 8 miles per hour. The engineer worked from one end and the fireman from the other end, an arrangement that dates to *Puffing Billy* in 1813–14. The locomotive pushed the tender, and as with many early locomotives and in keeping with British tradition, there was no cab. The unusual-looking locomotive had no frame; everything was just bolted to the boiler. With the vertical cylinders, it rocked from side to side as it waddled down the tracks.

The locomotive spent its working career transporting coal from mine to pier in the Stellarton and New Glasgow area for the Albion Mines Railway. It also saw some duty transporting passengers. *Samson* remained in regular service until 1867 and then continued to operate as needed until the mid-1880s.

Today, it can be seen in restored condition at the Nova Scotia Museum of Industry in Stellarton.

Sans Pareil replica

This Hackworth locomotive design clearly shows the vertical cylinders and linkage assembly without a frame or cab. The locomotive can be seen at the Locomotion Railway Museum in Shildon, United Kingdom.

JOHN MOLSON, 1840s

In 1832, John Molson began work on the Champlain & St. Lawrence Railroad to replace the slow and weather-impacted steamboat and stage service south of Montreal across Quebec into New York. The railroad began operation in 1836 with the *Dorchester*. Molson died in 1836, and in the late 1840s, a locomotive was named in his honor.

The *John Molson* was a 2-2-2 locomotive that was said to be the fastest in Canada at that time. It was built by Kinmonds, Hutton and Steel of Dundee, Scotland. The locomotive was designed for wood burning, and it operated across southern Quebec. It later became the property of the Grand Trunk Railway and is thought to have been retired in the mid-1870s. The current *John Molson* is a beautiful 1970 Kawasaki replica of the original. It is fully operational and used for demonstrations and educational purposes at Exporail, the Canadian National Railway Museum in Saint Constant, Quebec.

John Molson was an early example of a larger-driver locomotive. Larger drivers allowed for more speed without over-revving the locomotive drive train. Nowhere was this design better demonstrated than in Britain, and the 2-2-2 *Columbine* is a classic illustration. This locomotive balanced the boiler capacity, steam output, and piston power with the larger-driver design; otherwise, the large drivers were not effective. These locomotives were relatively tall, which compromised stability at high speeds.

By the mid-1800s, many American designs had further evolved by adopting a pivoting/leading wheel arrangement rather than the straight 2-2-2 arrangement that remained popular, especially in England. The pivoting/leading wheels essentially guided the drivers and the rest of the locomotive through turns and significantly reduced derailments while also supporting some of the engine's weight.

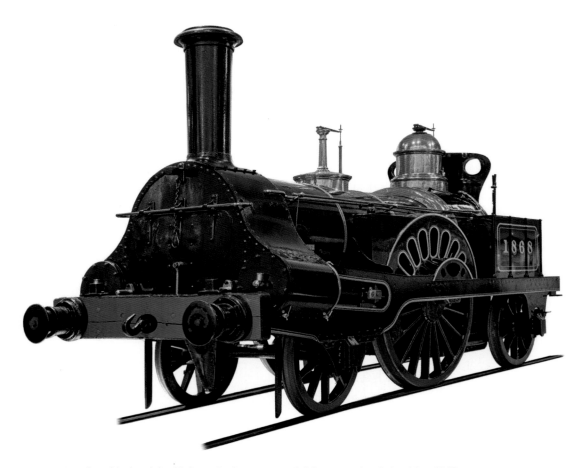

As with the *John Molson,* the large central drivers on the *Columbine,* 1845, allowed for more speed without over-revving the locomotive drive train. It is exhibited at the Science Museum in London.

Memnon, 1848
Baltimore & Ohio No. 57

Memnon was built for the Baltimore & Ohio in 1848 by Newcastle Manufacturing Company in Newcastle, Delaware (not to be confused with Robert Stephenson & Company in Newcastle, England). This locomotive was part of an overall order for six 0-8-0 locomotives that year, and *Memnon* was produced under sub-contract from Baldwin Locomotive Works. Although generally referred to as *Memnon*, the locomotive was also designated No. 57 and is sometimes called *Old War Horse* because of service rendered during the Civil War.

Memnon is one of the oldest surviving American freight locomotives and is also the only surviving Newcastle locomotive. It has been altered very little from its 1848 design, is in immaculate condition, and is an extremely important example of a rare mid-1800s North American locomotive. It was used to pull long coal and passenger trains. Most American locomotives from the mid-1800s era were woodburners, but *Memnon* burned coal.

The locomotive was rebuilt twice, in 1853 and 1884, but without major design changes, and it was retired in 1892. The engine was rebuilt again for display at the 1893 World's Columbian Exposition, and it last steamed at the 1927 Fair of the Iron Horse. *Memnon* is housed at the Baltimore & Ohio Railroad Museum, where the historic railroad was organized in 1827. The locomotive was damaged in the 2003 roundhouse roof collapse at the museum and restoration was completed in 2008.

One of the most revolutionary locomotive designs of the mid-19th century was the Crampton-type. Locomotive designers of this period wanted large-diameter driving wheels for speed and a low center of gravity for stability. With the drivers at the rear of the locomotive behind the low-mounted boiler, the Crampton provided both. Cramptons were built and tested in the United States over a period of about five years but failed because of the poor track quality at that time and the use of inadequate boilers and cylinders to power such large driving wheels. The *Le Continent*, 1852, with 7-foot drivers was a successful example in France. Contrast the *Le Continent* with the *Memnon*, which better met the requirements of period American railways.

THE CLASSIC, DEFINITIVE AMERICAN LOCOMOTIVE

By the mid-1800s, railroads had been extended to the grand waterways of the Ohio River, Mississippi River, and Great Lakes. In 1869, the first U.S. transcontinental railway was completed at Promontory Summit in Utah, with California Governor Leland Stanford driving the ceremonial golden spike.

One locomotive design, the 4-4-0 American-type, soon emerged as the most popular and important all across North America, and thousands were built. These locomotives were low in cost, reliable and versatile, and could run at high speeds over cheap, rough track.

During this era, industrial and agricultural economies were driven by the locomotive and the ability to move raw materials and products to market. Towns and cities sprang up all along the railroads.

In the Victorian tradition, the classic American steam locomotive developed into a superb machine with elaborate and colorful appointments.

Other locomotives were also designed and built specifically for tourist and recreational purposes.

LURAVILLE LOCOMOTIVE, CA 1850

This is possibly the oldest locomotive in the Deep South and the 4-4-0 American-type locomotive included in this historic photographic collection. It was built about 1850 by either Danforth Cooke & Company or by Rogers Locomotive & Machine Works. After several rebuilds, it is difficult to know which company built it originally, and a case can be made for either. This locomotive is a roughly 10-ton, woodburning engine with 62-inch drivers. It was likely purchased and brought into Florida for passenger and light freight service and was later sold into a second career in the extensive logging and forestry operations around Live Oak and Luraville, Florida; hence the name *Luraville*.

The *Luraville* spent 73 years at the bottom of the Suwanee River. (The Suwanee River was made famous by Stephen Foster in his song "Old Folks at Home" or "Way Down Upon the Swanee River.") The locomotive's immersion in the river probably saved it from being scrapped. During its later operating years, the locomotive was transported back and forth across the river on a barge as needed to work in logging operations on both sides. In 1906 (some accounts say 1898), during a routine crossing, the barge load became unbalanced, it capsized, and the engine was dumped into the Suwanee River. (Some accounts claim that the locomotive was rolled into the river intentionally by a bankrupt company or was lost while being loaded onto the barge.) It was not salvaged from the black waters of the live oak-lined river until 1979.

Today, the locomotive can be seen in very good restored cosmetic condition with a loaded logging car at the State of Florida Agriculture and Forestry offices in Tallahassee. The wooden cab and the homemade stack were built at shops in Lake City, Florida, and added in the mid-1980s as part of the restoration. The cowcatcher is missing.

A distinctive feature of the 19th century American locomotive is the cab, providing weather protection for the engineer and the fireman and adding style to the design. In contrast, many European locomotives from the era did not include a cab. The engineer or driver worked out in the elements much like the driver of a horse-drawn coach. In this way, it was argued that the crew would be more alert and attentive outside. The *Sezanne*, 1845, illustrates a typical European design, an approach that continued well into the last half of the century.

PIONEER, 1851

Built in 1851 by the Union Works in South Boston, Massachusetts, the *Pioneer* was built for the Cumberland Valley Railroad with operations in southern Pennsylvania and western Maryland.

The *Pioneer* is a small, 2-2-2T tank-type engine with one pair of relatively large driving wheels. It was used to pull short, light passenger trains of one to three cars, and it served very well in this capacity. The original construction was of wrought iron and cast iron with a wooden cab. The boiler was insulated with wooden strips and clad with lustrous and decorative metallic gray Russian sheet iron. Russian iron was very popular in locomotive construction during the mid- and late 1800s because it looked good where contemporary paints of the day could not survive the high temperatures on metal surfaces, especially on the smokebox and firebox. Because this is a tank engine, there is no tender, and water and wood were carried at the rear and below the locomotive's deck.

During the Civil War, the *Pioneer* carried troops and supplies for the Union Army. By the 1870s, the *Pioneer* could no longer pull the heavier railcars of the day, and it was relegated to work train and switching services. It officially retired in 1901 and was used in promotions and at trade shows.

The locomotive was donated to the Smithsonian Institute by Pennsylvania Railroad for exhibit beginning in 1963. In 2010, the Smithsonian Institute's National Museum of History and the Baltimore & Ohio Railroad Museum began an extensive restoration of the engine, which has now been completed. The *Pioneer* is currently on display at the Baltimore & Ohio Railroad Museum.

Pioneer shown in a side perspective view

General, 1855
Western & Atlantic No. 3

The *General* is, without doubt, one of the most famous locomotives in the world. Today, it is the main exhibit at the Southern Museum of Civil War and Locomotive History in Kennesaw, Georgia, near Atlanta. Officially, it is Western & Atlantic Railroad's 4-4-0 American-type locomotive No. 3, but it is universally known as the *General*. It was built by Rogers, Ketchum & Grosvenor in 1855 as a woodburning locomotive with 60-inch drivers and was originally painted green and orange. It was used for freight and passenger service between Chattanooga and Atlanta before the Civil War on the railroad's 5-foot gauge system.

In April 1862, the locomotive was commandeered at Big Shanty, Georgia, near what is now Kennesaw. Union raiders had plans to take the train north towards Chattanooga, destroy infrastructure along the way, and meet up with the advancing Union Army. An exciting 87-mile chase involving several locomotives ensued and continued until the *General* ran out of fuel and water and was overtaken by the *Texas*. The raiders were rounded up, and some were executed, and others were imprisoned. The *General* was towed back through Georgia by the *Texas*.

After the war, the locomotive resumed service until it was retired in 1891. It was cosmetically restored for the 1893 World's Columbian Exposition in Chicago and then was taken to Chattanooga, where it remained on display until the 1927 Fair of the Iron Horse in Baltimore, the 1933 Century of Progress Exhibition in Chicago, the 1939–1940 New York World's Fair, and the 1948 Chicago Railroad Fair. Louisville & Nashville Railroad restored the locomotive cosmetically and operationally in 1959 for the American Civil War Centennial, and it spent several years traveling to various events across the eastern United States, including the 1964 New York World's Fair. Interestingly, a long-running dispute between the City of Chattanooga and the State of Georgia over rights to the locomotive arose and was not settled until 1970 when the locomotive returned to Kennesaw, Georgia.

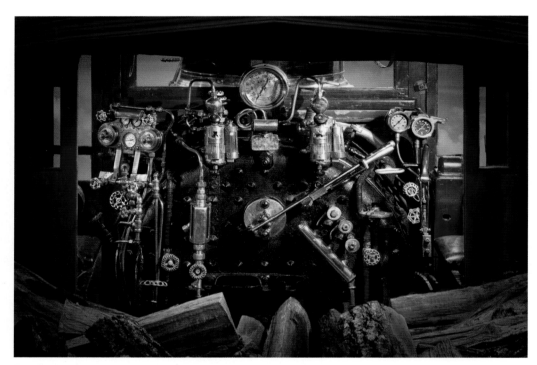

The *General*'s cab: originally the locomotive was designed for burning wood; it was later converted to coal and then to oil.

TEXAS, 1856
WESTERN & ATLANTIC NO. 49

The *Texas* is a beautiful 4-4-0 American-type, woodburning locomotive that was built in 1856 in Paterson, New Jersey, by Danforth, Cooke & Company for the Western & Atlantic Railroad. It cost about $9,000 at the time and was purchased as a freight engine. *Texas* was capable of speeds to 60 miles per hour and could travel 30 miles on a cord of wood. This was a 5-foot gauge locomotive with 60-inch drivers.

The *Texas* came to international renown as the winner of the 1862 Great Locomotive Chase in which a Confederate crew (led by William Fuller, conductor of the *General*) chased and recaptured the *General*, which was stolen by a band of Union agents (James Andrew's Raiders) in a daring race across northwest Georgia. The *Texas* chased the *General* in reverse for more than 50 miles (total chase was 87 miles and involved three locomotives) until the *General* ran out of fuel. The *Texas* towed the *General* back to the Atlanta area after the chase. The engineer on the *Texas* (Peter Bracken) was 28 years old, and the fireman (Henry Haney) was only 15 at the time of the chase.

After the war, the *Texas* returned to commercial service until 1903. In 1927, it was relocated to the basement of the Cyclorama Museum where it was restored to beautifully detailed condition. In 2015, the *Texas* was involved in a legal dispute between the State of Georgia and the City of Atlanta. The state wanted to move the *Texas* to the Southern Museum of Civil War and Locomotive History in Kennesaw where the *General* is located.

However, the courts ruled that the *Texas* belongs to the City of Atlanta. The *Texas* was then restored to its 1886 condition and moved to the Atlanta History Center in 2017. Today, the *Texas* and *General* are located in separate museums that are about 25 miles apart.

Some of the ornate Danforth, Cooke & Company detailing on the *Texas*

PRESIDENT, 1858

(ALSO KNOWN AS SAM HILL AND SATILLA)

The Victorian era of science, prosperity, and elegance emerged in Europe during the late 1830s, influencing the design of locomotives. During this time, some of the most beautiful locomotives ever designed came into service. The fashion spread across the Atlantic to inspire American locomotive designs such as the *General, Texas, Governor Stanford,* and *Daniel Nason* with their stained woods, ornate metals, fancy stacks and nameplates, brass trim, and elaborate paint schemes.

The *President* is classically elegant in the Victorian tradition. This 1858 4-4-0 American-type locomotive was built by Rogers Locomotive and Machine Works of Paterson, New Jersey, for the Atlantic & Gulf Railroad. It was a woodburning, standard gauge engine with 60-inch drivers that were later reduced to 55- or 53-inches in diameter.

As was the custom at that time, the locomotive was given a personal name, *Satilla,* for the Satilla River along the route of the Atlantic & Gulf in southern Georgia where it worked up to the Civil War. After the war, it continued to operate in Georgia until 1924 when Henry Ford bought it for his museum in Michigan. Ford renamed it *Sam Hill* for a Michigan Central Railroad engineer he knew in the Dearborn area when he was a child.

The third and current name for the locomotive is *President* in honor of President Herbert Hoover. The locomotive was used to transport the Herbert Hoover presidential party to Dearborn to celebrate the opening of the Henry Ford Museum and Greenfield Village in 1929. Today, *President* is displayed in the museum and still bears two names: *Sam Hill* and *President.*

The *Saint Pierre,* 1844, is the oldest original locomotive in continental Europe. It clearly illustrates early Victorian-era design elements.

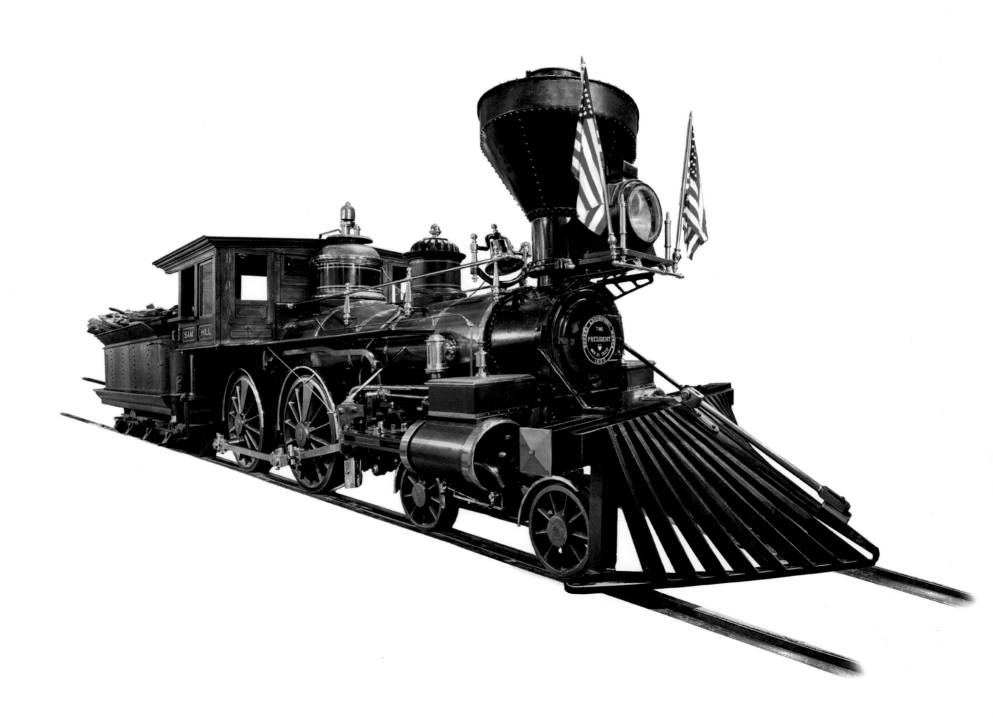

Daniel Nason, 1858
Boston & Providence Railroad No. 17

Daniel Nason is a unique and treasured American industrial artifact. The design is very distinctive. It is the oldest steam locomotive in the collection at the Museum of Transportation in St. Louis, Missouri. This locomotive was built in Boston by Roxbury Locomotive Works in 1858 with some refinements continuing until 1863. Although the 4-4-0 wheel arrangement was popular during this era, this is the only surviving American-type locomotive with the cylinders and main driving rods located inside the locomotive frame, contributing to its distinctive appearance. The locomotive weighs in at over 52,000 pounds and has 54-inch drive wheels and 30-inch leading truck wheels.

Locomotives with inside cylinder design were common in Europe and were cleverly known as "Insiders." Visually, the locomotive, as displayed in St. Louis, has been backdated with a large woodburner chimney, even though it is a coal burner.

Daniel Nason was one of 28 locomotives produced under the direction of George Griggs, generally considered one of the most important locomotive designers in American history. His locomotives were known not only for their excellent performance but also for their handsome design elements. *Daniel Nason* was displayed in several major exhibits, including the 1893 World Columbian Exposition in Chicago and the 1939–1940 World's Fair in New York.

George Griggs, the designer of *Daniel Nason*, wanted his locomotives to be good pullers and good lookers. While the *Daniel Nason* is a 4-4-0 American-type locomotive, it shares some design elements with European locomotives, most notably the inside cylinders, as illustrated on British Furness Railway No. 20.

Governor Leland Stanford, 1862
Central Pacific No. 1

The mid-19th century in California's gold rush country was a notable era in American history. San Francisco, Sacramento, Sutter's Mill, and the Sierras were the settings for getting rich, starting a new life, raising a family, going into business or suffering hardship, disappointment, and even death. Local railroads were incorporated in California as early as 1852, but any railroad equipment had to be shipped in by sea around Cape Horn. Dreams of a transcontinental railroad were a decade or more away in a country consumed by political strife and ultimately war during this era.

The Central Pacific Railroad was authorized by Congress in 1862 and the first rails were laid in 1863 to begin the Transcontinental Railroad. The Central Pacific's first locomotive was Central Pacific Railroad No. 1, popularly known as *Governor Leland Stanford*, named for a railroad financier, the first president of the railroad, and a former governor of California.

This beautiful 40-ton, woodburning 4-4-0 American-type locomotive was built during the Civil War in 1862 by Norris Locomotive Works and transported by ship 19,000 miles, in disassembled form, around South America for delivery in California.

Governor Leland Stanford was used for passenger and freight service and was involved in the construction of the Transcontinental Railroad, which was completed at Promontory Summit, Utah, in 1869. Central Pacific president Leland Stanford was at Promontory to drive in the ceremonial final spike.

Governor Leland Stanford is now displayed in immaculate, 1899 condition at California State Railroad Museum in Sacramento. The original 1862 condition was not possible as part of the restoration because the boiler and cylinders had been rebuilt and enlarged in 1878.

Mariposa/Stockton Terminal & Eastern Railroad No. 1, 1864

About two years after *Governor Stanford* was delivered, Norris Locomotive Works built this 4-4-0 American-type locomotive named *Mariposa* for the Western Pacific Railroad. The locomotive turned out to be a workhorse and operated almost continuously from 1864 until 1953 for Western Pacific, Central Pacific, Southern Pacific, and finally for Stockton Terminal & Eastern Railroad. It can be examined at Travel Town in Los Angeles.

C. P. Huntington, 1863
Southern Pacific No. 1

The *C. P. Huntington* is possibly the most significant and celebrated locomotive across the northern California region. For years, it was the symbol for the Southern Pacific and made numerous promotional appearances for the railroad over more than half a century. An outline of the locomotive is currently featured on the logo of the California State Railroad Museum. It was named for Colin P. Huntington, the third president of the Southern Pacific holding company.

C. P. Huntington is a small, 4-2-4T, oil-burning tank engine with an extended tending area behind the cab. Oil-burning locomotives and railroad oil service facilities became popular in the Southwest, where coal mines were hundreds or even several thousand miles away. As oil became more available in the early 20th century, more and more steam locomotives made the conversion from wood and coal to oil.

This is the only surviving standard gauge 4-2-4 locomotive in the United States. The locomotive was built for the Central Pacific by Danforth, Cooke & Company in Paterson, New Jersey, in 1863 and shipped around Cape Horn. It has a "bicycle" wheel arrangement, with only two drivers providing limited traction. The railroad wanted a larger engine, but with the Civil War raging, nothing larger was available. It was initially used in the construction of the Transcontinental Railroad from the west and was transferred to the Southern Pacific in 1871, where it pulled passenger trains and was used in maintenance work, right-of-way burning, and construction projects in northern California.

The engine was refurbished in 1970 at the Sacramento Shops and rebuilt by the California State Railroad Museum in 1980. It is now on prominent display in beautiful 1914 condition at this museum in Sacramento.

C. P. Huntington's oil-fired locomotive cab

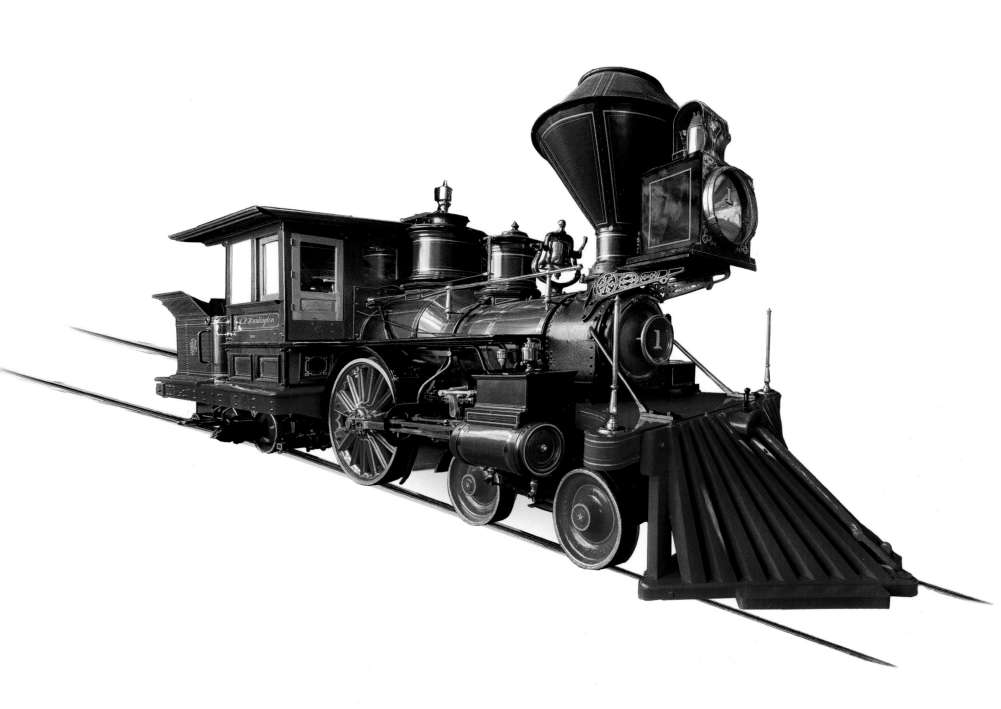

THATCHER PERKINS, 1863
BALTIMORE & OHIO NO. 147

When the Civil War broke out, the Baltimore & Ohio Railroad had equipment and operations spread across both northern and southern states. Locomotives were taken over by the armies, and much equipment was lost or destroyed during the conflict. Thatcher Perkins, who was Baltimore & Ohio's master of machinery at the time, recommended that the Baltimore & Ohio build several Ten-Wheeler locomotives as replacements for the lost and destroyed engines. These Perkins-designed engines proved to be exceptional in both operation and design and performed extremely well over several decades of service.

First named No. 147, *Thatcher Perkins* was built in 1863 at the Mt. Clare shops near Baltimore as a coal-burning, 4-6-0 Ten-Wheeler. It was used in both freight and passenger service over routes through the Appalachian Mountains and was described as well balanced and reliable in operation. The locomotive is 53 feet long overall and weighs 90,700 pounds. The locomotive was selected for preservation by the railroad in 1892 to be used for public relations and exhibition purposes. It was designated *Thatcher Perkins* in 1927 during the Fair of the Iron Horse event in Baltimore.

This locomotive was one of several that were severely damaged when the Baltimore & Ohio museum's roundhouse roof collapsed in 2003 during a heavy snowstorm. Extensive and meticulous restoration was undertaken by the staff at the museum. *Thatcher Perkins* is truly beautiful in Indian red, vermillion, dark gray, black, and brass and is classically outfitted with American flags. This locomotive is featured in a number of books on railroading and locomotives.

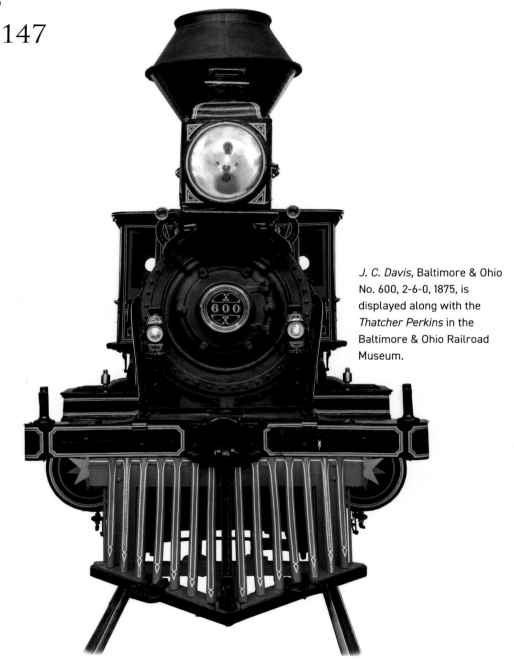

J. C. Davis, Baltimore & Ohio No. 600, 2-6-0, 1875, is displayed along with the *Thatcher Perkins* in the Baltimore & Ohio Railroad Museum.

Peppersass, 1866
Mount Washingtion Railway No. 1

In July 1869, *Peppersass* ascended Mount Washington and became the world's first operational cog railway locomotive. It was built by Campbell, Whittier & Company in Massachusetts in 1866 and was originally named *Hero* and is often referred to as *The Old Hero*. The name was later changed to *Peppersass* because it resembled a bottle of pepper sauce.

Like many other early locomotives, *Peppersass* featured a vertical boiler, although somewhat angled for incline operation. The inclined vertical boiler helped to ensure that water covered the crown sheet in the firebox on the steep mountain grades to avoid an explosion. *Peppersass* is based on a simple chassis and frame concept, and the engineer stood outside on a platform, with no cab. This locomotive had a coal-fired design.

In addition to providing commercial service, *Peppersass* was used in the construction of the cog railway. Beginning in 1878, soon after the railway was completed, the locomotive went on a lengthy traveling promotional exhibition.

In 1929, it was restored for commemorative operation at the 60th anniversary of the railroad. During the trip up the mountain, the front axle broke and one member of the crew was killed and several people were injured as the locomotive raced down the mountain and crashed. *Peppersass* was retired from routine duties after this tragic event but the pieces were reassembled. It is now on display at the railroad's base station.

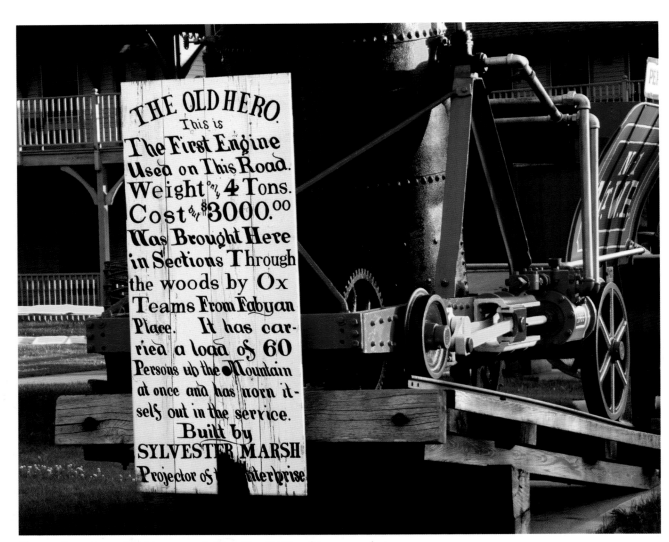

Signage from Mount Washington explaining *The Old Hero* (*Peppersass*) story

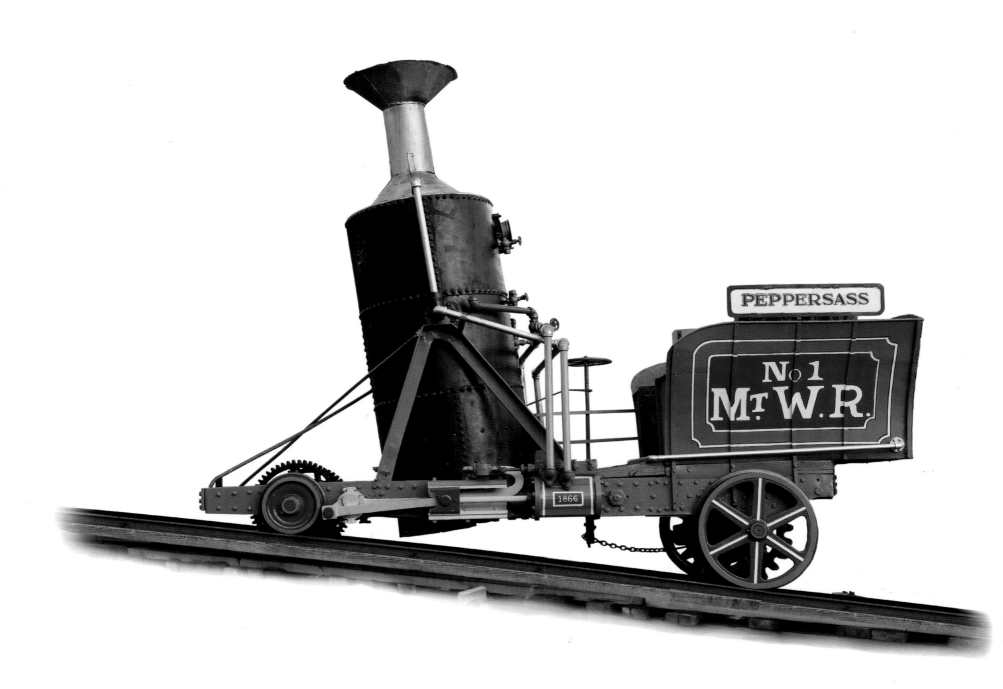

BALTIMORE & OHIO NO. 305, 1869

(CAMEL LOCOMOTIVE)

This beautiful, unusual and historic locomotive is a 4-6-0, coal-burning design that was built at the Baltimore & Ohio's Mt. Claire Shops in 1869. The design became known as the Davis Camel after the designer and location of the engineer perched high and above the boiler like on the back of a camel. The concept was to provide more room for a larger coal-burning firebox by relocating the traditional cab at the back of the locomotive to a position above the boiler. This put the engineer directly over the hot boiler and the fireman was left standing in the weather at the front of the tender. The arrangement did provide great visibility for the engineer, but communication with the fireman was limited and it was a very uncomfortable and dangerous design.

About 100 Davis Camels were built. Production was discontinued in the 1870s as locomotive materials and designs evolved and the enlarged firebox was no longer necessary to produce the energy needed to power the locomotive.

After retirement, No. 305/217 attended a number of events, exhibitions, shows, and fairs. At some point number 217 was applied, but historians do not think the number was ever used in actual service or operation.

Significantly, the locomotive was severely damaged in the 2003 Baltimore & Ohio Roundhouse roof collapse but has been meticulously restored to its original Indian red, black, and gold coloring and markings with number 305. It is now displayed at the Baltimore & Ohio Railroad Museum.

Baltimore & Ohio No. 305 was No. 217 when this image was taken around 1980.

MINNETONKA, 1870
NORTHERN PACIFIC NO. 1

The Northern Pacific Railroad was chartered by Congress in 1864 to develop a rail line from Minnesota to the Pacific Ocean across the northern regions of the United States and to connect the Great Lakes with Puget Sound on the Pacific. This development would open vast new areas of the nation for farming, logging, and mining. *Minnetonka* was one of the first four locomotives purchased by Northern Pacific to be used for construction on the line.

The small locomotive was shipped in pieces around Cape Horn and reassembled in Washington for work on the western end of the railroad. Some accounts indicate that all or part of the locomotive may have actually been shipped by rail to San Francisco and from there loaded on a ship for transport to Washington.

The *Minnetonka* is an 1870 vintage Smith & Porter 0-4-0T tank-type woodburner that was built in Pittsburgh, Pennsylvania. In 1886, it was sold to a logging company. Ultimately, it was retired in the 1920s and abandoned somewhere in the Northwest. Northern Pacific personnel later found the locomotive sitting in a wooded area, recognized its value, and traded a working locomotive for it. It was apparently still operable and the railroad employed it for exhibitions over several decades.

Ultimately, the railroad found a final home for it in Minnesota where it is on display alongside the 1861 *William Crooks*. Since 1975, the two remarkable locomotives have been exhibited at the Lake Superior Railroad Museum in the historic Duluth Union Station.

William Crooks, Great Northern Railroad No. 1, 1861, is displayed with *Minnetonka* at the Lake Superior Railroad Museum.

RENO, 1872
VIRGINIA & TRUCKEE NO. 11

Visit Old Tucson Studios near Tucson, Arizona, and one of the most remarkable and prominent displays is Virginia & Truckee Railroad No. 11. This historic locomotive is commonly known as *Reno*, although in recent decades it has been temporarily renamed for various movie roles. *Reno* is a 4-4-0 woodburner, and it is one of the most photographed locomotives in the world. It was built by Baldwin Locomotive Works in 1872 and was originally owned and operated by the Virginia & Truckee. *Reno* was, and is, a classic picturesque western 4-4-0 American-type locomotive, which hauled more than $400 million in gold and silver from the Comstock Lode.

The locomotive operated at an exciting time in the Old West, primarily for express passenger service in the Reno and Virginia City area. It carried several American icons including President Ulysses S. Grant, President Theodore Roosevelt, Union General William Tecumseh Sherman, and circus legend P. T. Barnum. This was an exquisitely ornate locomotive in its heyday with all the era's detailing and appointments of brass, molding, and polish. Today, it is the oldest surviving Virginia & Truckee locomotive.

Reno has appeared in more than 100 films at Old Tucson, including movies starring John Wayne, Katherine Hepburn, Paul Newman, Barbara Stanwyck, and Clint Eastwood. There is considerable interest in additional restoration for this historic locomotive.

In an Old West setting, *Reno* is seen below Sentinel Peak near Old Tucson, Arizona.

Torch Lake, 1873
Calumet & Hecla Mining Company No. 3

This 1873 Mason Bogie or Mason-Fairlie tank locomotive was built by the William Mason Machine Works in Taunton, Massachusetts. The *Torch Lake* name comes from the earlier mining company name of Hecla & Torch Lake Railroad. Of the many Mason locomotives built to this design, No. 3 is the only remaining example in the world. Visually, *Torch Lake* is a very stylish locomotive.

Fairlie locomotives were conceived and patented by Robert Fairlie in 1864. *Torch Lake* is a single-ended Fairlie, while the more familiar Fairlie design was double-ended, like the *Livingston Thompson*. Fairlie-Patent locomotives could make sharp turns because their trucks could swivel under the engine, much like the trucks swivel under a modern diesel-electric locomotive. To the Fairlie design, William Mason Machine Works added classic refinements.

Torch Lake was used in the copper mining country of Michigan's Upper Peninsula for both mainline and switching work. It was retired and placed into storage by Calumet & Hecla Mining Company in 1933 after more than 50 years of service. In 1966, No. 3 became part of the Calumet & Hecla centennial celebration, and it was then donated to the Edison Institute, which is now the Henry Ford Museum. The locomotive arrived at Greenfield Village in 1970. Before it could be operated, the boiler, firebox and steam dome were replaced, and it was converted from wood to oil firing. In 1971, it began pulling passenger cars at the village.

Compared with *Torch Lake*, the 1886 *Livingston Thompson* was a much more exotic, double-ended, narrow gauge Robert Fairlie-design locomotive with cylinders and swiveling powered bogies at each end. It had no tender and it carried water and coal in locomotive bunkers down each side of the engine. It is on display at the National Railway Museum, York, United Kingdom.

TAHOE, 1875
VIRGINIA & TRUCKEE NO. 20

With the discovery of silver and gold in northwest Nevada, the corridor between Virginia City and Carson City quickly became overrun with rail traffic, and a number of locomotives were ordered by Virginia & Truckee. Nine of these locomotives remain today. *Tahoe*, Virginia & Truckee No. 20, is one of the survivors. It was built by Baldwin Locomotive Works in 1875. This 2-6-0 Mogul-type engine was a woodburner and relatively powerful for the time.

Tahoe was later rebuilt for coal firing in 1907 and then converted to oil in 1911. *Tahoe* went into storage in 1926 but was later sold in 1942 and used in construction during World War II. In 1968, it was purchased by the Railroad Museum of Pennsylvania.

About 11,000 Mogul-type locomotives were built between 1860 and 1900, primarily for relatively low-speed freight operations. With only two leading wheels and more weight distribution to the rear, Moguls tended to derail more frequently than their American-type counterparts, limiting the top speed for safety considerations.

Another famous Virginia & Truckee Mogul-type locomotive is *Empire*, or Virginia & Truckee No. 13. It was also converted to oil during the same period as the *Tahoe* conversion.

Empire, Virginia & Truckee No. 13, 1873, is on display at the California State Railroad Museum.

EDISON No. 1, 1870s

Edison No. 1 is familiar to anyone who has visited Greenfield Village at the Henry Ford Museum in Dearborn, Michigan. This beautiful little locomotive was displayed inside at the museum from 1932 until the early 1960s and was then moved next door to the village for regular service on the tourist railroad that traverses the property.

The origins of this locomotive have been a source of some confusion over the years. *Edison* dates to the 1870s and was built by Manchester Locomotive Works in Manchester, New Hampshire, where the steam cog locomotives for Mount Washington were built. It was originally an 0-4-0 design that burned oil. The locomotive belonged to Thomas Edison and was used in quarry operations. Edison gave the locomotive as a gift to his friend Henry Ford in the early 1930s. Ford envisioned a more "Old West" American-type look and had it rebuilt as a 4-4-0 in 1932. He wanted something with a William Mason locomotive appearance. (*Daniel Nason* is an example.)

Over the years, the locomotive has been converted from oil to coal, and the original balloon stack was replaced first with a diamond chimney and later with a straight stack. A new metal cab was added, along with a metal cowcatcher, and colorful paint and brass have been introduced. In more recent years, additional mechanical safety work has been done, the boiler has been replaced, and the compressor, valve, and brake systems upgraded.

Edison No. 1, under steam, rolls into the roundhouse at Greenfield Village.

Ammonoosuc, 1875
Mount Washington Railway No. 2

Manchester Locomotive Works built this coal-fired cog locomotive in 1875. It was named *Atlas* and assigned No. 4. This was the ninth locomotive to work on the slopes of Mount Washington, which has an average grade of more than 25 percent and a maximum grade exceeding 37 percent. Following a fire in 1895, the engine was rebuilt, renumbered as engine No. 2, and the name *Atlas* was dropped.

In 1931, as locomotive No. 2, it was named *Ammonoosuc*, and amazingly, it is still in excellent operational condition today. No. 2 consumes about a ton of coal and 1,000 gallons of water over the 3-mile trip up the mountain as the temperature drops 20–30°F or more. This locomotive generates a lot of smoke, but it is exempt from New Hampshire air pollution control laws, as are all other locomotives built before 1973.

Conventional, friction-based locomotives and railways are not designed for operation on steep grades. Locomotives under load cannot typically pull a train up a grade of more than 4 or 5 percent and cannot safely descend a steep grade, even at low speeds and with sand added to the track for traction. Although grades as steep as 7–10 percent are sometimes quoted for friction railways, actual percentages on mainline railroads are realistically more like 3–4 percent maximum. Steeper grades require either cog (rack-and-pinion) or cable systems for dependable and safe operation.

A dramatic view of the Mount Washington cog railway

SONOMA, 1876
NORTH PACIFIC COAST NO. 12

In the decades following the California gold rush, rail lines opened and locomotives ran frequently north of San Francisco into Napa and Sonoma. One of these locomotives was *Sonoma*, No. 12. This narrow gauge 4-4-0 American-type, oil-fired locomotive was built by Baldwin Locomotive Works in 1876. It is assumed to have been used, along with two other Baldwin locomotives, for both passenger and freight service.

Sonoma was sold to Nevada Central Railroad in 1879, where it worked until 1938 when the railroad went bankrupt. At Nevada Central, it was renamed *General Ledlie* and assigned number 5. There, it was used for yard and construction projects as well as railway operations.

In 1938, the locomotive was loaned to the Railway & Locomotive Historical Society, Pacific Coast Chapter. It was taken to the Southern Pacific shops and backdated for an Old West appearance to look as much as possible like Central Pacific's *Jupiter*, one of the locomotives from the 1869 golden spike ceremony that completed the first Transcontinental Railroad. With this appearance, *Sonoma* became part of the daily Transcontinental Railroad reenactment at Golden Gate Park for the 1939 San Francisco International Exposition, with a follow-up exposition in Sacramento during 1940.

From 1940 until 1977, it was stored in the Sacramento area until it was donated to the California State Railroad Museum in 1978. By using Baldwin drawings and specifications, *Sonoma* has been restored to its original factory appearance and is displayed beautifully with a set of period passenger cars in the museum's Great Hall.

Here's *Sonoma*, North Pacific Coast Railroad No. 12, 1876, in a perspective view.

NEVADA SHORT LINE NO. 1, 1879

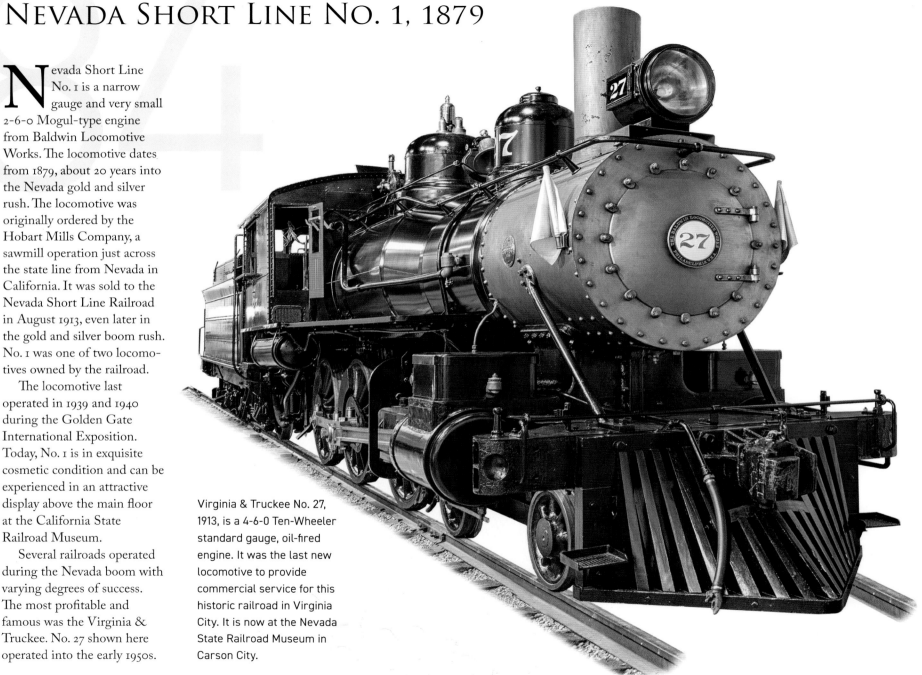

Nevada Short Line No. 1 is a narrow gauge and very small 2-6-0 Mogul-type engine from Baldwin Locomotive Works. The locomotive dates from 1879, about 20 years into the Nevada gold and silver rush. The locomotive was originally ordered by the Hobart Mills Company, a sawmill operation just across the state line from Nevada in California. It was sold to the Nevada Short Line Railroad in August 1913, even later in the gold and silver boom rush. No. 1 was one of two locomotives owned by the railroad.

The locomotive last operated in 1939 and 1940 during the Golden Gate International Exposition. Today, No. 1 is in exquisite cosmetic condition and can be experienced in an attractive display above the main floor at the California State Railroad Museum.

Several railroads operated during the Nevada boom with varying degrees of success. The most profitable and famous was the Virginia & Truckee. No. 27 shown here operated into the early 1950s.

Virginia & Truckee No. 27, 1913, is a 4-6-0 Ten-Wheeler standard gauge, oil-fired engine. It was the last new locomotive to provide commercial service for this historic railroad in Virginia City. It is now at the Nevada State Railroad Museum in Carson City.

STEAM
ACROSS
AMERICA

Through the closing decades of the 1800s, the steam locomotive continued to evolve. The American-type locomotive grew larger, and alternate wheel configurations were investigated to support heavier engines and meet specialized requirements.

Almost every city and town in America and many in Canada were served by rail. Locomotives became more reliable, dependable, and safer. Standard time zones were introduced in 1883 to facilitate scheduling. In 1885, the first transcontinental rail line was completed across Canada by Canadian Pacific Railway.

Denver, South Park & Pacific No. 191, 1880

This is the oldest authentic locomotive in Colorado, a state with many remarkable steam locomotives and a very colorful railroading past—and present—steam culture. It was built in 1880 by Baldwin Locomotive Works as a 2-8-0 Consolidation-type, coal-fired, narrow gauge engine and was numbered 51 until 1885, when it became No. 191.

No. 191 was the second of an order of eight Consolidation-type locomotives, the largest engines yet built for the Denver, South Park & Pacific. These were very early Consolidation locomotives in an era dominated by American-type designs. It weighs almost 62,000 pounds but has eight relatively small 37-inch driving wheels for low-speed freight and ore-hauling operations. The locomotive was used in mining ventures through central Colorado for 22 years during and after the mineral rush.

In 1899, it was sold to a lumber company in Wisconsin and remained there until it was acquired by the Colorado Railroad Museum in 1973. No. 191 is one of two surviving Denver, South Park & Pacific locomotives. It can be seen and appreciated at the extensive Colorado Railroad Museum in Golden. The other remaining Denver, South Park & Pacific locomotive is preserved at Breckenridge.

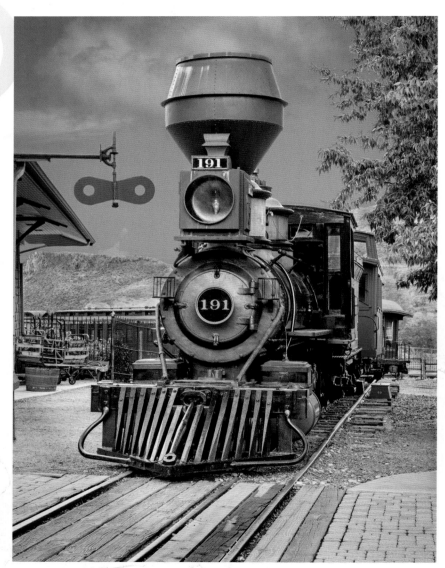

Denver, South Park & Pacific No. 191, 1880

BOTWOOD RAILWAY NO. 7, 1881

(TANK LOCOMOTIVE)

This tiny 0-6-0 tank-type engine was built by Hawthorn Leslie and Company in England and brought to Newfoundland for the construction of the Newfoundland Railway. It operated on 42-inch gauge with just 27-inch drivers, and it was coal-fired. The design was copied by the smaller American locomotive manufacturers.

By about 1908, No. 7 had been acquired by Botwood Railway, where it was used to transport pulp, paper, and other wood products between Grand Falls and Bishop's Fall and Botwood on the coast for shipping. It did see some limited passenger service, although it is difficult to envision how such a small locomotive with no tender could travel very far without taking on additional water and coal. By about 1938 or 1940, the paper mill placed the locomotive on a siding and basically discarded it to be scrapped later.

A group of concerned citizens saw the plight of the little engine and rescued it for historical preservation. Today, Botwood Railway No. 7 is prominently displayed at the Mary March Museum in Grand Falls, Newfoundland.

Bauxite, 1874 (Hebburn Works No. 2)

Another historic example of a small tank-type locomotive from the same era is this 0-4-0T Black Hawthorn & Company engine that was used in British aluminum smelter work. It is at the National Railway Museum in York, United Kingdom

MADISON, 1881
W. T. SMITH LUMBER COMPANY NO. 14

Madison is the oldest surviving locomotive in Alabama and one of the oldest in the Deep South. It was built in 1881 by Baldwin Locomotive Works during the Burnham, Parry, Williams & Company era (1873–1890) at Baldwin for the Central Railroad & Banking Company of Georgia. As was traditional at this time, the locomotive was named *Madison* and assigned No. 109. It was built as a 5-foot gauge engine but was converted to standard gauge in 1886.

When the railroad reorganized as the Central of Georgia Railway in 1895, the locomotive became No. 1501, and it was sold to Birmingham Rail & Locomotive Company. A succession of sales and owners followed, first to Buck Creek Lumber Company, then to Empire Lumber Company, and finally to W. T. Smith Lumber Company. For all three of these companies, the locomotive was known as No. 14, probably to avoid the cost and effort of relettering.

Union Camp Corporation purchased W. T. Smith Lumber Company in 1966. The locomotive was subsequently donated for exhibit at the Pike Pioneer Museum in Troy, Alabama. It sat for a number of years in Chapman, Alabama, near the Smith lumber mill but is now preserved under cover at the museum. The *Madison* has 57-inch drivers, weighs about 70,000 pounds, and was always operated with coal.

Glover Machine Works Locomotive No. 4, 1916

Glover was the largest and last locomotive builder in the Deep South. After the Civil War, Glover began manufacturing custom steam-powered machinery and repairing locomotives. From this expertise, the company ultimately built about 200 locomotives before ending production in 1930. Glover factory machinery is now displayed at the Southern Museum for Locomotive and Civil War History in Kennesaw, Georgia.

Satsop Railroad Company No. 1, 1885

(Tank Locomotive)

Satsop Railroad No. 1 (named for a group of Native Americans from the Olympic Mountains region) was the first conventional, rod-driven linkage steam locomotive to arrive in the Northwest, and it was used extensively for assorted logging, hauling, and switching assignments.

The locomotive was ordered from H. K. Porter in Pittsburgh, Pennsylvania, in 1885 as an 0-4-2T tank-type engine. It was designed to burn coal and operate on standard gauge track. At 14 tons, it was relatively small even by the standards of that era. Over about 60 years of service, it was owned by several timber and logging companies and was renamed and renumbered multiple times. It was originally named *Currie* and then *C. F. White*.

As with most Porter locomotives, this is a very functional and durable machine and does not have an ornate or flashy design. The current cab is fairly spacious, and the paint colors make for a delightful appearance with red, gold, and green trim.

After retirement, No. 1 was initially put on display and then rebuilt for operation. Later, it again returned to display and was ultimately donated to what is now the Mount Rainier Scenic Railroad, where it was treated to an extensive cosmetic restoration. At the railroad museum in Mineral, Washington, the locomotive is used as an educational and interactive exhibit.

A cab view of Satsop Railroad No. 1

BLACK DIAMOND, 1889

(INSPECTION LOCOMOTIVE)

Historically, an inspection locomotive was a small steam engine used primarily for transporting railroad executives, management, civil engineers, and a few other passengers to examine construction sites, review road work, and perform a range of other railroad activities. Then, as today, they were considered a bit odd by outsiders and railroads that did not really use or understand them. Some were luxurious and others were rebuilt from existing and obsolete small locomotive engines with modified passenger car bodies mounted on top. They looked a little like the dummy locomotives and trolley cars of the day but were configured inside for business and some were plush in appointment.

The only surviving inspection locomotive in the United States today appears to be the Reading Company's *Black Diamond*, which was built in 1889 by Baldwin Locomotive Works. This tiny 2-2-2 steam engine features a leather box seat and four additional leather swivel seats with walnut woodwork, French plate glass, and nickel-plated hardware. The interior is so tight on space around the boiler that a small boy was said to be required as the fireman. The exterior is painted in raw umber and gold, and the wheels are red with a red pilot. The *Black Diamond* was used for almost 20 years and then retired around 1908 but was kept by Reading for various special occasions.

In 1948, Reading agreed to lend the locomotive to the Museum of Transportation in St. Louis in what, by some accounts, was thought to be a donation. When Reading became part of Conrail in 1976, the Reading archives were examined and the loan of the *Black Diamond* was discovered. The trustees of Conrail wanted the locomotive returned, but the Museum of Transportation did not want to give up the classic little engine. Negotiations followed and a price of $5,000 in Proctor & Gamble stock was agreed upon and a bill of sale to the Museum of Transportation was signed for the *Black Diamond* in 1979. Today, it can be seen in the main locomotive pavilion at the museum with fresh paint, lettering, and logos.

A perspective view of *Black Diamond*

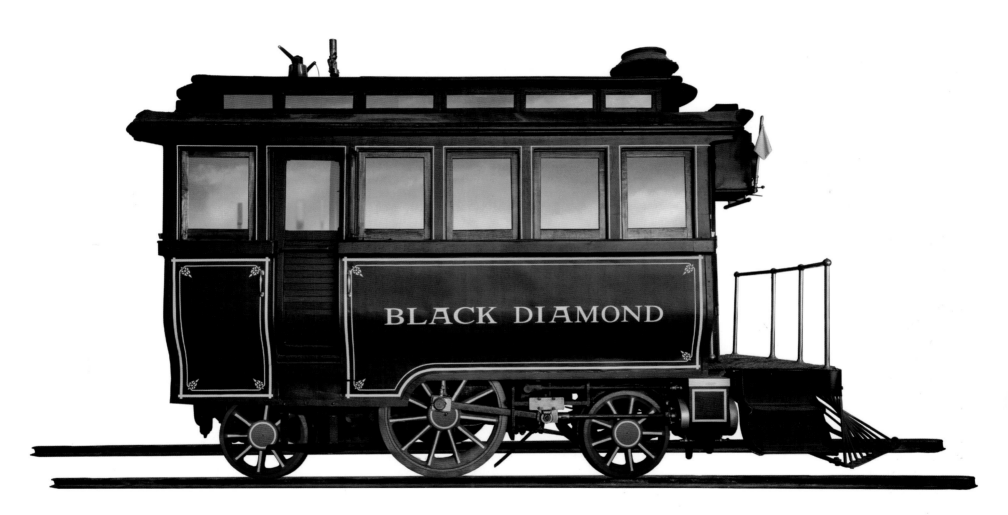

CENTRAL OF GEORGIA NO. 349, 1891

No. 349 is a classic 4-4-0 American-type locomotive of the late 1800s. It was built for the Savannah & Western Railroad by Baldwin Locomotive Works. By the early 1890s, the American locomotive had grown relatively large and powerful, and No. 349 weighs in at over 101,000 pounds as a standard gauge, coal-fired engine. Historically, the locomotive became part of the Central of Georgia Railway when the Savannah & Western was consolidated with six other railroads in 1895.

Today, No. 349 has been cosmetically restored and stands at the entrance to the very active Tennessee Valley Railroad Museum in Chattanooga. The engine is striking in appearance with a bright red Central of Georgia logo, red cab roof and trim, and red number plate. The cab interior is restored to excellent display condition.

Central of Georgia No. 349's coal-fired locomotive cab

Manitou & Pike's Peak Railroad No. 1, 1891

In 1891, this became the first locomotive to climb Pikes Peak from Manitou Springs in central Colorado and reach the 14,110-foot summit. The locomotive was built by Baldwin Locomotive Works and is a coal-fired, 0-4-2 cog-type locomotive designed to climb the 16 percent grade on the mountain. Altogether, the railway owned and operated six steam cog locomotives. No. 1 through No. 5 all had an 0-4-2 wheel arrangement and burned coal. No. 6 had an 0-6-2 wheel arrangement and burned oil.

These locomotives were designed to maintain a relatively level boiler for the steep incline of the mountain and ensure dependable performance. Notice the Vauclain compound cylinder arrangement, which reduced fuel and water consumption.

Beginning in 1938, the railway switched to gasoline- and diesel-powered locomotives. Only No. 4 from the original steam locomotive fleet is currently operational. No. 1 can be seen at the Colorado Railroad Museum in Golden.

A rack system (developed by Carl Roman Abt) is used for the Pike's Peak railway track. This design is based on two side-by-side steel racks with multiple sets of alternating upward-pointing teeth that engage with the locomotive's drive wheel/ cog for smooth, nonslip movement up and down the steep grade. The maximum grade for the rack system is about 25 percent.

Italian cog locomotive No. R370 023, 1921

In the United States, cog locomotives were limited primarily to tourist service and a few other specialized applications. Across mountainous regions of central and southern Europe, cog locomotives were fairly common through the mid-20th century to provide both passenger and freight service.

BOSTON & MAINE NO. 494, 1892

Boston & Maine Railroad No. 494 was built at the Manchester Locomotive Works, best known for producing the historic cogged steam locomotives used on Mount Washington Railway. It is one of only a few surviving Manchester locomotives and may be the only surviving 4-4-0 American-type locomotive, although ruins of what is thought to be a Manchester American-type were dug from the mud in Florida around 2012. No. 494 was originally ordered by Eastern Railroad and came to Boston & Maine in 1911. It was used for pulling passenger trains and light freight trains and ended its working career by hauling coal.

No. 494 was cosmetically restored for the 1939–1940 New York World's Fair, where it was displayed along with a *Tom Thumb* replica and the Pennsylvania Railroad S1, which was designed by Raymond Loewy. The restoration work included backdating in an attempt to provide an authentic 1892 locomotive. The electric generator and head-light, metal cab, and other updates were removed as part of the backdating.

After the fair, No. 494 was stored for a number of years and was almost scrapped. It was saved by a group called The Railroad Enthusiasts. They found a display location in 1957 for the locomotive at White River Junction, Vermont. Today, the locomotive features a teal-colored boiler, graphite-colored stack and smokebox, polished and painted linkage, and a complete and labeled wooden cab. Additional restoration is underway by the Friends of 494, and meanwhile, No. 494 is displayed with a tender and caboose under cover at the White River Junction station.

In the historic Mount Washington area, coal would have been delivered by Boston & Maine locomotives. Waumbek No. 9, shown in this image, was built by Manchester Locomotive Works in 1908.

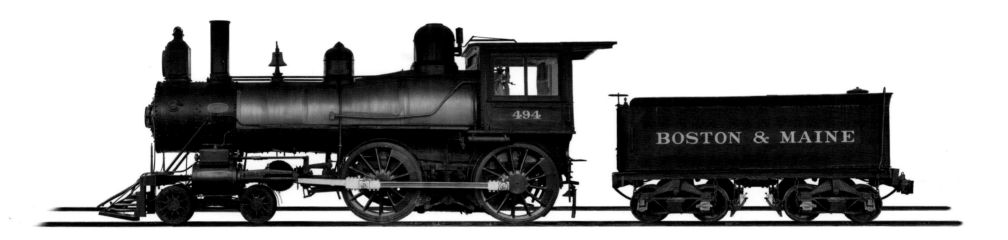

Queen of Speed, 1893
New York Central & Hudson River No. 999

In the late 1800s, competition between New York Central and the Pennsylvania Railroad was intense, especially on the routes between New York City and Chicago. With the coming of the 1893 World Columbian Exposition (Chicago World's Fair), each railroad wanted to claim the fastest service. New York Central developed a plan to refine locomotive No. 999, a handmade, 37-foot, American-type 4-4-0 locomotive, with a goal of attaining a speed of 100 miles per hour. The railroad installed 86-inch-diameter driving wheels rather than the usual 70-inch wheels, refitted linkage along with 2-foot piston travel, and added special brakes for safety. Cosmetically, the engine was impressive with a black satin finish; highly polished trim, bands, and pipes; and gold-leaf lettering.

On May 10, 1893, while pulling the *Empire State Express* passenger train, a speed of 112 miles per hour was calculated over a portion of track between Rochester to Buffalo, but the speed could not be positively and officially confirmed, and the train speed recorder only indicated 86 miles per hour. Did the locomotive actually reach the claimed speed of 112 miles per hour? Most experts do not think so. Regardless, the locomotive was fast and became known as the *Queen of Speed*. It was considered by many to be the first to reach 100 miles per hour. No. 999 became instantly famous and toured the nation.

Later, the *Queen of Speed*'s 86-inch drivers were replaced with smaller 70-inch wheels, the boiler was exchanged, and the engine was relegated to branch line and switching operations. It was restored for the Baltimore & Ohio's 1927 Fair of the Iron Horse and also exhibited at the World's Fair in New York in 1939–1940. It was retired in 1952 and then donated to the Chicago Museum of Science and Industry in 1962, where today it is a popular and featured exhibit inside the museum's main hall.

The *Queen of Speed*'s cab

A 1901 commemorative stamp features the *Empire State Express*, referred to on the stamp as *East Express*.

PENNSYLVANIA RAILROAD NO. 7002/8063, 1902

In 1905, about a decade after the famous 100-mile-per-hour run by the *Queen of Speed,* Pennsylvania Railroad began a new 18-hour high-speed train service from New York City to Chicago to compete with similar service offered by the New York Central. On June 11, 1905, Pennsylvania Railroad No. 7002 en route to Chicago and near Elida, Ohio, in two separate observations, was clocked at nearly 127.1 miles per hour, although not by officially documented speed indicators.

To the later embarrassment of Pennsylvania Railroad, locomotive No. 7002 was scrapped in the mid-1930s. For the 1939–1940 New York World's Fair and some railroad events, Pennsylvania Railroad took No. 8063, which was from the same general class of locomotives and also built in 1902, renumbered it, and modified it too look as much as possible like No. 7002. The renumbered engine was displayed as the world's fastest steam locomotive. Some differences between the two locomotives remained.

Both the original No. 7002 and No. 8063 were 4-4-2, coal-fired Atlantic-type engines from the Pennsylvania's Altoona Works. A large firebox, high steam pressure, and 80-inch drivers contributed to high-speed operation. These were both very fast passenger locomotives, but they never achieved the notoriety of the New York Central's *Queen of Speed*, which made its famous run in 1893.

In 1979, the locomotive was donated to the Railroad Museum of Pennsylvania, where it was used by the Strasburg Rail Road for hauling short rides and excursions, sometimes as a doubleheader with Pennsylvania Railroad No. 1223. Both these locomotives were later removed from service and placed on display inside the museum after testing indicated that their boilers and fireboxes did not meet safety standards.

City of Truro, 1903, is famous as the "other" first locomotive to reach 100 miles per hour while hauling a load. As with the *Queen of Speed* and Pennsylvania Railroad No. 7002, the actual speed of the *City of Truro* is disputed, but the fact that all of these locomotives were incredibly fast has never been a subject of debate. The famous speed run took place in the United Kingdom in 1904.

DETROIT & LIMA NORTHERN RAILWAY NO. 7, 1897

This magnificent 4-4-0, coal-burning American-type locomotive was completed by the Baldwin Locomotive Works in Philadelphia in 1897 and delivered to the Detroit & Lima Northern Railway, which later became the Detroit Southern Railway and then the Detroit Toledo & Ironton. The locomotive was built for passenger service.

Henry Ford purchased the Detroit Toledo & Ironton in 1920 and transformed it into an efficient and profitable operation. He built an extensive new shop (Fordson Shop) to refurbish the railroad's 80 locomotives and accompanying rolling stock. No. 7 was the first locomotive to be overhauled. The engine was disassembled, and parts were inspected and replaced. Cosmetics were also part of the rework. Iron was replaced with copper, the boiler jacket was lacquered, and the drivers were painted white.

Ford and his friends Thomas Edison and Harvey Firestone personally used the locomotive. In 1929, Ford sold the railway to the Pennsylvania Railroad but kept No. 7. The next year, another restoration of No. 7 began, and the locomotive was donated to the Edison Institute, which became the Henry Ford Museum. It was displayed in the museum until 1985 and then was placed in a train shed.

In 1997, an evaluation began to determine if the locomotive could be brought back to operating condition for use at Greenfield Village. The restoration was completed in 2013, including modification to allow the large American-type locomotive to negotiate the tight turns at the village. Today, the locomotive is striking with a dark green cab, Russian iron jacketing, and extensive gold and red hand-painted trim.

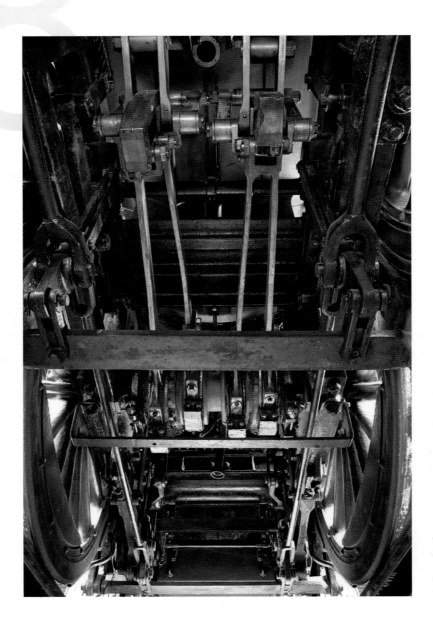

This view is from beneath Detroit, Toledo & Ironton No. 45 (4-4-2 Atlantic-type wheel arrangement) at the Henry Ford Museum.

GOLDEN AGE OF THE LOCOMOTIVE

As the 20th century approached, the locomotive entered its golden age. Although American-type locomotives were still in demand, larger and faster designs were needed to meet the growing need for moving ever more passengers and increasing freight loads. Passenger traffic peaked for most railroads in about 1920 with more than 50,000 steam locomotives in service.

Locomotive manufacture became increasingly the work of a few large builders. American Locomotive Company, Baldwin Locomotive Works, and Lima Locomotive Works dominated the locomotive market with a range of concepts and designs. European locomotives continued to influence American designs and vice versa.

Fascinating geared locomotives were working at logging and construction sites across the continent. Electric locomotive technology was emerging and demonstrating the advantages of quick starts, good traction, and cleaner operations.

MINNEAPOLIS, ST. PAUL & SAULT STE. MARIE NO. 2645, 1900

Built as No. 247 for Wisconsin Central Railroad, this 4-6-0 Ten-Wheeler is a classic example of a Brooks Locomotive Works engine just before the operation merged into American Locomotive Company in 1901. With 57-inch drivers and beautiful cosmetics, this engine spent its entire working career in Wisconsin.

After display, first in a park and later at a former rail station in Wisconsin, No. 2645 was donated in 1988 to the Mid-Continent Railway Museum. At the museum, it has been cosmetically restored and is displayed with a colorful lineup of classic freight cars. The coal-burning engine remains a great candidate for mechanical restoration. The size, weight, and styling are perfect for historic operations at almost any rail museum.

Dating to 1883, Minneapolis, St. Paul & Sault Ste. Marie in 1961 officially took on the "Soo Line" name, at the same time merging with Wisconsin Central and Duluth, South Shore & Atlantic. Controlled by Canadian Pacific since the late 1800s, CP acquired full ownership in the early 1990s.

Soo Line No. 2645 is shown at North Freedom Station, Mid Continent Railway Museum, Wisconsin.
(The smoke and steam have been added for effect, as the locomotive is not operational.)

E. E. BIGGE, 1900
OLD SYDNEY COLLIERIES NO. 25

In 1900, the Nova Scotia Steel & Coal Company ordered No. 25 from Baldwin Locomotive Works in Philadelphia, Pennsylvania, to support area mining operations around Sydney Harbor on Cape Breton Island. This order was for an unusual 2-4-0T tank-type, standard gauge, coal-fired maritime locomotive. It was named *E. E. Bigge* in honor of a British General Mining Association director and immediately went to work carrying supplies, equipment, and crews around the mining work areas. The locomotive has 16 x 24-inch cylinders and 54-inch drivers. It operated at 120 pounds of boiler pressure and weighed about 85,000 pounds with its tender.

Although built as a tank engine, the side tanks were removed in 1910 to increase fuel capacity, and a wooden-frame tender was added. During 62 years of hard work, the engine mostly handled coal hopper cars and provided daily commuter service for the miners at shift change.

Later, as the company dieselized, No. 25 was relegated to coal-washing operations. As sister units were scrapped, this locomotive was saved because it had been promised to the National Railway Museum (Exporail) as representative of early colliery locomotives in the Maritime Provinces. As of 2015, it is prominently displayed atop a massive truss podium at the entrance to Exporail National Railway Museum south of Montreal, Quebec.

Rockton & Rion Railway No. 20 / Mount Yonah's steam locomotive, 1904

This American Locomotive Company 0-4-0T tank-type engine can be seen along Highway 75 near a bookstore south of Helen, Georgia. The large green tank or "saddle" on No. 20 is an obvious and unique feature of the tank-type locomotive. *E. E. Bigge* was also built as a tank-type locomotive, although the tanks were later removed.

ILLINOIS CENTRAL NO. 790, 1903

No. 790 was built in 1903, along with three sister locomotives, by the Cooke Works of the American Locomotive Company for Chicago Union Transfer Railway. The only remaining Chicago Union Transfer locomotive, it was sold to Illinois Central in 1904. This is a 2-8-0 Consolidation-type locomotive and was used primarily as a heavy freight engine. As would be expected, this is a standard gauge, coal-fired engine, and it runs on 51-inch drivers and weighs in at 183,000 pounds. Superheating was added in 1918.

This locomotive survived, in part, because it was needed on several occasions to assist with Mississippi River floodwater relief where diesel-electric locomotives could not be used in the high water. It was considered for excursion work in the 1960s and became part of the Steamtown National Historic Site collection in 1966. Today, No. 790 can be enjoyed in excellent cosmetic condition at the site in Scranton, Pennsylvania.

Beginning in the mid-1800s, the American locomotive industry evolved through the 4-4-0 American, 2-6-0 Mogul, 4-6-0 Ten-Wheeler, 4-4-2 Atlantic, 2-8-0 Consolidation, 4-6-2 Pacific, and other designs in search of a universal locomotive. Similar evolutions occurred in other countries, and it is interesting to see this progression, as shown for France (pictured).

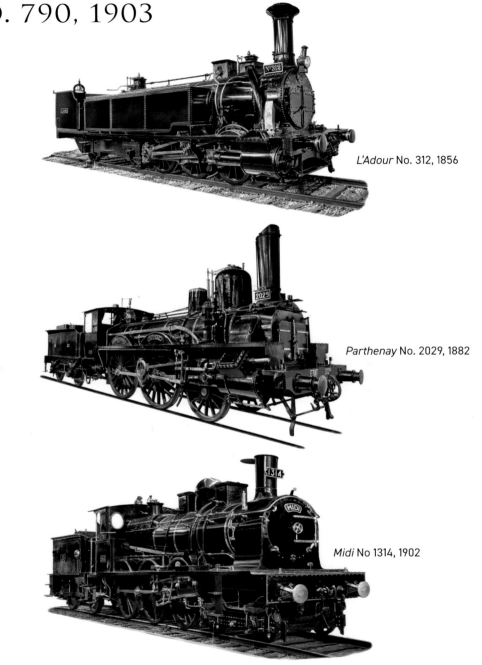

L'Adour No. 312, 1856

Parthenay No. 2029, 1882

Midi No 1314, 1902

SHARON STEEL HOOP COMPANY NO. 4, 1904
HUNTSVILLE RAILWAY COMPANY NO. 4

Sharon Steel Hoop Company No. 4 is a small 0-4-0, standard gauge, coal-fired locomotive built by H. K. Porter in 1904. The locomotive spent its early years at a steel mill in Sharon, Pennsylvania, where the company made steel hoops, bands, and ties. When the company expanded through acquisition, the locomotive was relocated to Lowellville, Ohio.

In 1963, No. 4 was sold to Sam Conti of Ohio and was restored and modified by Lakecraft Corporation for amusement park operations. The locomotive came to Huntsville, Alabama, in 1985, when it was purchased by the city for display at their Huntsville Depot Museum. As a part of the preparation for display, the locomotive was cosmetically restored and became Huntsville Railway Company No. 4.

H. K. Porter began producing locomotives in 1866 in Pittsburgh, not far from the Sharon Steel Hoop mill. By the time its locomotive operations ceased in 1950, Porter had become the largest producer of industrial and specialty locomotives in America. Almost 8,000 locomotives rolled out of the Porter shops, and many survive today.

Huntsville Depot Museum was built in 1860 as a passenger station and railroad office.

PENNSYLVANIA RAILROAD NO. 1223, 1905

Pennsylvania Railroad No. 1223 is a stunning example of a "modern" 4-4-0 American-type locomotive. It was built at the railroad's Juniata Shops in Altoona, Pennsylvania, late in the American-type era as a high-speed passenger engine with tall driving wheels and clean, attractive styling. By 1905, when the locomotive began commercial operation, American-type locomotives were already being replaced in passenger service by larger and more powerful Atlantic- and Pacific-type engines. Steel passenger cars were becoming popular at the time, and they were just too heavy for even the most modernized 4-4-0 engine.

To extend the useful life of No. 1223, the tall 68-inch drivers were replaced with smaller wheels, improved piston valves and superheating were fitted, and other modifications were made to adapt the locomotive for freight work. As a result, No. 1223 became one of the last three Americans working on the Pennsylvania Railroad.

Because the style of the locomotive was so appealing, No. 1223 was selected for display at railroad fairs over a period of several decades beginning in the 1930s, and it was subsequently chosen for preservation. This locomotive sits on prominent display near Pennsylvania Railroad No. 7002 at the Railroad Museum of Pennsylvania in Strasburg near Lancaster.

In 1969, No. 1223 made a signature appearance in the movie *Hello Dolly* with Barbara Streisand and Walther Matthau. The movie essentially opens in an amazing sequence of glamorous cinematography of the locomotive traveling along the Hudson River.

Because Pennsylvania Railroad was such a large and dominant operation in the Northeast, other smaller railroads looked for any advantage to compete. One effective approach was faster service. An example was Central Railroad of New Jersey No. 592, a very fast 1901 Camelback 4-4-2 Atlantic-type locomotive that could reach speeds of up to 90 miles per hour and was often used on competitive passenger routes. It is seen here on display at the Baltimore & Ohio Railroad Museum.

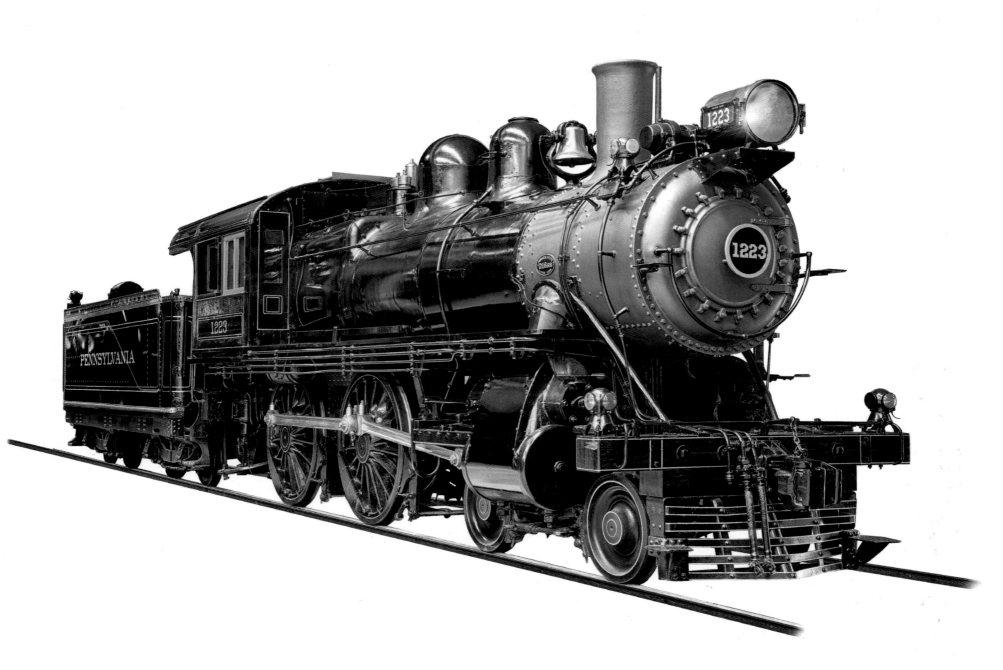

SOUTHERN RAILWAY NO. 630, 1904, AND NO. 4501, 1911

No. 630 is a coal-fired locomotive built in 1904 by American Locomotive Company in Richmond, Virginia. It has a 2-8-0 wheel arrangement, so it is referred to as a Consolidation-type locomotive. No. 630 worked on Southern Railway in freight service, including short haul and yard work, until 1952 when it was retired and sold. After being sold, bought, leased, and loaned a number of times over the years, the locomotive was donated to the Tennessee Valley Railroad Museum in 1999. At the museum, it underwent an extensive decade-long restoration, including frame and drive gear rework, and returned to service in 2011 for steam excursions. Since that time, the locomotive has been used by the museum around Chattanooga and also as part of the 21st Century Steam Program making excursions across the Southeast.

No. 4501 was built by Baldwin Locomotive Works in 1911 as a 2-8-2 Mikado-type engine. After it was retired in 1948, it was purchased by Kentucky & Tennessee Railway. In 1963, the locomotive was retired again and moved to Chattanooga for restoration at the Tennessee Valley Railroad Museum, where it was part of the Southern Railway excursion program until 1994 and was taken out of service in 1998. After extensive restoration work, No. 4501 passed the U.S. Federal Railroad Administration boiler and certification tests and began excursion service in the fall of 2014. Southern Railway No. 4501 is famous as the original locomotive used in the Southern Railway steam excursion program beginning in 1966. This locomotive has also appeared in several movies and a Johnny Cash music video.

Southern Railway No. 630 and No. 4501 as a doubleheader rolls across northern Georgia.

GREENBRIER & ELK RIVER / CASS SCENIC NO. 5, 1905
(SHAY LOCOMOTIVE)

With almost the intricacy of a clockwork mechanism, Shay locomotives, built by Lima Locomotive Works, are among the most fascinating machines ever built. These geared steam locomotives feature precision vertical cylinders and a long horizontal articulated crankshaft with multiple powered/geared trucks. The crankshaft includes universal joints for maneuvering through tight turns and up and down steep hills. All wheels, including those under the tender, are typically powered to maximize traction. The horizontal boiler is offset to one side, typically the left, opposite the gearing and crankshaft for balance.

Competing geared locomotives included designs by Heisler and Climax and later Willamette, but the Shays were first to the market and the most popular and most numerous. About 3,500 Shays were built by Lima before production ended in 1945. All four geared locomotive designs were optimized for logging and also for construction and other heavy applications that involved temporary and poor quality track, steep grades, and tight turns with low-speed operation.

Lima built the first Shay in 1880. It was invented by Ephraim Shay, who was a schoolteacher and merchant turned logger and inventor. Patents were granted in 1881 and 1901. At first, Lima, a machine works business, was not excited about the concept, but over time, Shay locomotives distinguished Lima as one of the largest and most prestigious locomotive companies in the world. No. 5 is a C-80 Shay in which the C indicates three cylinders and the 80 stands for 80 tons, although some specs show No. 5 as a 90-ton engine. It was built in 1905, making it one of the oldest locomotives in the world in continuous service on the same railway and the second oldest Shay in existence.

Shay geared locomotives at Cass, West Virginia

Orange Blossom Cannonball, 1907
Tavares, Eustis & Gulf No. 2

The *Orange Blossom Cannonball* is a standard gauge, woodburning, 2-6-0 Mogul-type engine built by the Baldwin Locomotive Works in 1907. The locomotive operates on 47-inch drivers and at 180 pounds per square inch of boiler pressure. Over the years, it has served Luftkin Land & Lumber Company, Shreveport, Houston & Gulf Railroad, Carter-Kelley Lumber Company, W. T. Carter & Brother Lumber Company, Scott & Bearskin Lake Railroad, and Reader Railroad.

Since 1964, the locomotive has appeared in more than 20 television and movie projects starring some of Hollywood's most famous actors, including Natalie Wood, Robert Redford, Charles Bronson, Slim Pickens, Jeff Bridges, Gregory Peck, Patrick Swayze, Linda Evans, Renee Zellweger, George Clooney, James Coburn, Christian Bale, Matt Damon, and Holly Hunter. This locomotive's movie résumé includes *True Grit, 3:10 to Yuma, There Will Be Blood, Oh Brother, Where Art Thou?,* and *Abraham Lincoln: Vampire Hunter.*

Today, old No. 2 is better known as the *Orange Blossom Cannonball.* Since 2011, the locomotive has made regular excursions between Tavares and Mt. Dora in north central Florida for the Tavares, Eustis & Gulf Railroad. The passenger cars pulled by the *Orange Blossom Cannonball* were 1915-vintage wooden carriages built for the Memphis, Dallas & Gulf Railroad, which is now part of Kansas City Southern.

Orange Blossom Cannonball's woodburning cab

Chattanooga Choo Choo, 1910
Cincinnati Southern No. 29

In 1942, Glenn Miller received the first gold record in history for the big band swing song "Chattanooga Choo Choo," which remained at number one on the Billboard charts for nine weeks in 1941. It was also nominated for an Academy Award as best song and is now in the Grammy Hall of Fame. The song tells a story about traveling by train from New York City to Chattanooga, Tennessee. Historically, Chattanooga had been a major rail center for many years, with the first trains entering the city in 1849. The location along the Tennessee River and at the base of Lookout Mountain was strategic for travel and transportation even in Native American times.

In the 1850s, Chattanooga began to develop into a railroad town and was of tactical railway importance throughout the Civil War. After the war, rail lines were extended from the city deep into the South with connections to cities across the Northeast and to the West. In 1880, passenger service opened from Cincinnati to Chattanooga and the route became popularly known as the Chattanooga Choo Choo.

Cincinnati Southern Railroad No. 29 (now named *Chattanooga Choo Choo*) can be seen on the tracks behind the world-famous Chattanooga Choo Choo terminal station complex near downtown Chattanooga. This locomotive came to Chattanooga in the early 1970s from a region farther north in Tennessee where it had been used in dam construction. Now brightly painted and in very good display condition, it was built in 1910 by Baldwin Locomotive Works. It is a 2-6-0 Mogul-type, coal-fired locomotive.

The East Chattanooga Station is busy with vintage locomotives. (from the Tennessee Valley Railroad Museum)

Shawnigan Lake Lumber Company No. 2, 1910–1911

(Climax Locomotive)

In addition to Shay geared logging and construction locomotives, Climax and Heisler locomotives were two additional major national competitors in that sector. The Climax locomotive was patented in 1891 and built in Corry, Pennsylvania. Climax locomotives were generally characterized by 25-degree slanted cylinders, one on each side, that were linked to a transmission and driveshaft connected to the axles through bevel gearing. Both two-truck and three-truck designs were built, and the models were designated Class A, B, or C, with the Class A vertical cylinder models being the smallest. Climax salesmen claimed that their locomotives were "more balanced" and less damaging to rails than a Shay because the driveshaft ran down the middle of the chassis rather than on one side.

More than one thousand units were produced over about a 40-year period ending in the late 1920s. At the peak of production, 17 different versions were available. The Class B two-truck models received the most positive reviews from users and were popular with logging, mining, bricklaying, and industrial switching operations. About 20 Climax locomotives remain today in various states of repair.

Shawnigan Lake Lumber Company No. 2 is in gorgeous, museum-quality display condition and is preserved inside the main museum at the British Columbia Forest Discovery Center in Duncan. A historical plate on the locomotive indicates that it was built in 1911, although other records show 1910. It is a Class B 25-ton, two-truck machine that worked west of Duncan in the Cowichan Lake region until it was abandoned in the woods in 1927. It stayed there until 1970, when it was reclaimed and moved out of the woods. In 1975, the locomotive was fully refurbished to operational condition at the Caycuse Shops of British Columbia Forest Products. It was subsequently donated to the Province of British Columbia.

Mayo Lumber Company No. 3, 1924 (Class B Shay locomotive), and Hillcrest Lumber Company No. 9, 1915 (Class B Climax locomotive), illustrate competing technologies in the yard at the British Columbia Forest Discovery Center.

EASTERN ARIZONA RAILWAY NO. 3, 1917
CRAIG MOUNTAIN LUMBER COMPANY NO. 3

(TWO-TRUCK HEISLER LOCOMOTIVE)

This fascinating steam locomotive is a 1917, two-truck geared locomotive built by Heisler Locomotive Works in Erie, Pennsylvania. The Heisler geared locomotive design featured two cylinders at 45-degree angles to form a V-twin drive arrangement. Power was transmitted through a driveshaft under the locomotive to propel the outside axle on each powered truck through beveled gears in an enclosed differential or gear case on the axle between the truck frames. The inboard axle on each truck was then driven from the outboard one by external side connecting linkage. This design was well suited to logging, construction, and other railroad applications in which torque and power were needed.

The Heisler design was patented by Charles Heisler in 1892. It featured a central boiler and better balance in operation than the competing and more popular Shay design. Heislers were marketed as a faster alternative if a little more speed was needed at a logging or construction site. Heisler advertising stated that Shay locomotives were more damaging to rails on the right side with the vertical cylinders, but this statement does not appear to be proven in actual operating situations. Also, with Heislers, the gearing was located inside the frame, where it was better protected and less exposed to damage than with Shays. Eastern Arizona Railway No. 3 can be seen on display at Alamosa Station near the Rio Grande River in the San Luis Valley region of Colorado. This standard gauge engine ran on oil.

About 625 Heisler locomotives were built, first by Dunkirk Engineering Company and then by Stearns Locomotive Company which became the Heisler Locomotive Works. Production ended in 1941.

Geared locomotive designs:

Heisler

Shay

Climax

PICKERING LUMBER COMPANY NO. 2, 1918

(THREE-TRUCK HEISLER LOCOMOTIVE)

No. 2 is a 1918 three-truck type Heisler locomotive with angled, side-mounted cylinders and geared driveshaft linkage to all three trucks. As all geared locomotives, this Heisler was built and used for construction, logging, timber work, and other high-stress service.

The Heisler design was in direct competition with the Shay, Climax, and Willamette geared locomotive designs. Heisler was the fastest of the geared locomotives. Both the Shay and Climax designs were more popular in terms of total sales. The Willamette geared locomotives were primarily limited to the Northwest, and only 33 were ever produced.

With all four geared locomotive designs, the tender rides on a pulling truck to improve traction. Heisler, Shay, and Climax designs can be seen at Cass Scenic Railroad in West Virginia, at the Railroad Museum of Pennsylvania, Mount Rainier Scenic Railroad, and several other historic railroading sites. Fewer than 40 Heislers remain today.

No. 2 was originally built for the Hetch Hetchy Railroad and was used in dam and aquaduct construction in California. This particular Heisler is a standard gauge, oil-fired engine that weighs about 150,000 pounds. No. 2 is a rare and historically significant locomotive. It is now owned by Travel Town, where it is on display at Griffith Park in Los Angeles.

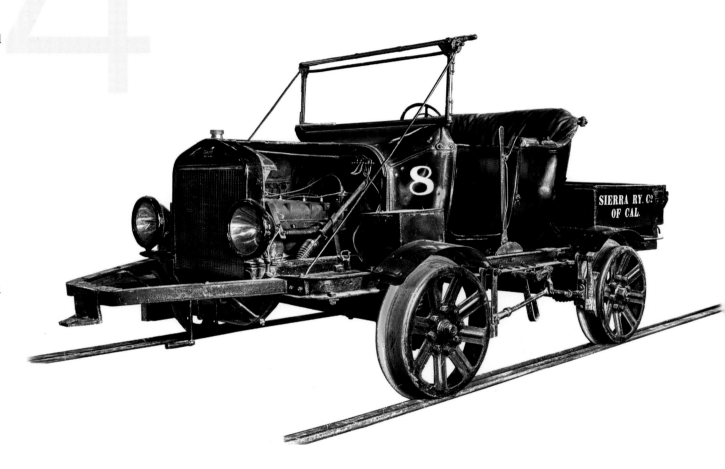

Sierra Railway of California No. 8, 1922

This vintage two-seat railcar was fabricated from a Ford Model T on a Fairbanks-Morse frame and used for inspections and distribution of employee pay at construction sites in the Sierras, where geared locomotives would have worked. It was made famous by actress Olivia de Havilland in the 1939 film *Dodge City*. It is now at Railtown 1897.

CHEROKEE BRICK & TILE COMPANY NO. 1, 1920

(COLUMBIA-TYPE LOCOMOTIVE)

Cherokee Brick & Tile Company No. 1 is a rare 2-4-2 Columbia-type locomotive that was designed for industrial and switching applications. The *Columbia* name was coined because Baldwin Locomotive Works submitted a locomotive of this wheel arrangement as one of the first entries at the 1893 Columbian Exhibition in Chicago to commemorate the 400th anniversary of Columbus. The 2-4-2 wheel arrangement was never very popular.

No. 1 was built by H. K. Porter in 1920 as a small tank-type locomotive for Cherokee Brick & Tile Company, and it operated in Macon, Georgia. The locomotive's saddle water tanks were later removed and the tender was added to create an unusual design. The locomotive operated until the early 1970s, most recently in South Carolina for rail enthusiasts. After retirement, it next became part of the collection at the Tennessee Valley Railroad Museum.

Today, the locomotive is the centerpiece of the Cowan Railroad Museum in Tennessee, where it is displayed in excellent cosmetic condition between the historic depot and the CSX main line leading to the steep 2 percent grade that crosses the Cumberland Plateau through the Cowan Tunnel. This is an important main line that has required helper engines for more than 150 years.

Sumter & Choctaw Railroad No. 102, 1924

As another example of a diminutive locomotive, this was the smallest standard gauge 2-8-2 Mikado-type locomotive ever built. It is on display at the National Railway Museum, Green Bay, Wisconsin.

NEWFOUNDLAND RAILWAY NO. 593, 1921
CANADIAN NATIONAL NO. 593

Newfoundland Railway No. 593 is a 4-6-2, 42-inch narrow gauge steam locomotive built by Baldwin Locomotive Works in early 1921 as No. 193. The coal-fired locomotive sits on 52-inch drivers and weighs about 116,000 pounds. Newfoundland Railway No. 593 operated for 36 years and logged 1.5 million miles across the rocky island. It is the finest remaining steam locomotive in Newfoundland and can be enjoyed at the Humbermouth Station along the waterfront as a feature of the Corner Brook Railway Museum. Several sister locomotives were scrapped in 1957 and 1958.

The first locomotive and railway operations in Newfoundland date to 1881 on what became the Newfoundland Railway. The tracks were 42-inch gauge and characterized by steep grades and sharp curves with snow and ice issues throughout the winter. At 906 miles, the Newfoundland Railway was the longest narrow gauge line in North America.

When Newfoundland became a Canadian province in 1949, the rail line was added to the Canadian National network. Locomotives were renamed and renumbered. Canadian National made significant infrastructure upgrades, including major work to the mainland shipping terminal at Port aux Basque where narrow and standard gauge bogies were switched. The last trains ran in Newfoundland in 1988.

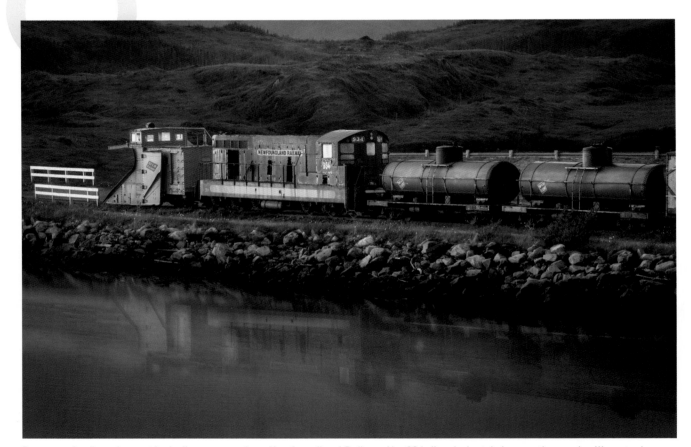

Preserved rail equipment including a snowplow, Newfoundland Railway No. 934 diesel-electric locomotive, and rolling stock are on display at Port aux Basque.

GRAND CANYON RAILWAY NO. 4960, 1923

In 1901, the Atchison, Topeka & Santa Fe began rail service to the Grand Canyon from its main line in Williams, Arizona. Over the decades that followed, the automobile eroded the railway business until passenger service was discontinued in 1968. In 1989, passenger service resumed as the Grand Canyon Railway, this time as a tourist railroad with hundreds of passengers traveling to and from the canyon each day. Since service restarted, a mix of diesel-electric and steam locomotives have been used over the 60-plus mile run with much more diesel-electric than steam motive power in recent years. The railroad maintains two exquisite steam locomotives, No. 4960 and No. 29, but primarily operates vintage diesel-electric engines on the run to and from the canyon.

No. 4960 is a 2-8-2 Mikado-type locomotive that was built by Baldwin Locomotive Works in Philadelphia in 1923 to post-World War I United States Railroad Administration standards. It operated as a freight and coal-hauling engine for the Chicago, Burlington & Quincy until the late 1950s and, after restoration, began service on the Grand Canyon Railway in 1996. No. 4960 has 64-inch drivers and weighs almost 311,000 pounds.

The stablemate of No. 4960, No. 29, is a 2-8-0 Consolidation-type locomotive built in 1906 by American Locomotive Company in Pittsburgh. The engine operated on the Lake Superior & Ishpeming Railroad across Michigan's northern peninsula in both passenger and freight service. It has 50-inch drivers and weighs over 219,800 pounds. No. 29 was restored in 2004 at a cost of more than $1 million and 26,000 man-hours of labor. When not in actual operation, the locomotives are often displayed alongside the former Santa Fe station in Williams. Both can now operate on low-sulfur fuel oil or vegetable oil.

Grand Canyon Railway No. 29, 1906

Woodward Iron Company No. 38, 1924

No. 38 is a small 2-8-0 Consolidation-type steam locomotive of the scale commonly used by American railroads for freight service between the 1880s and the 1920s. By the 1930s, the railroads needed larger and more powerful engines, and locomotives like No. 38 were relegated to branch line and switching work. No. 38 was built by Baldwin Locomotive Works in 1924 for short hauls and switching on the property of Woodward Iron in Birmingham, Alabama.

During the early 1950s, the locomotive was sold to B&H Lumber Company and then donated to the Heart of Dixie Railroad Museum in the 1960s. It weighs in at 186,000 pounds and has 50-inch drivers. No. 38 is a popular attraction with train enthusiasts and photographers, and it can be seen on display in excellent condition at Heart of Dixie Railroad Museum in Calera, Alabama.

In 1881, Woodard Iron Company began operation in the rich iron ore fields of Alabama across an area that was rapidly developing into the City of Birmingham. By the 1920s, Woodward Iron was one of the nation's largest suppliers of pig iron and employed several thousand workers in mines, blast furnaces, and rail operations. The company operated its own railroad along the face of Red Mountain to access the ore mines and deliver raw materials to its furnaces and foundries. Woodward ceased operations and sold some properties in the early 1970s as the demand for steel products declined.

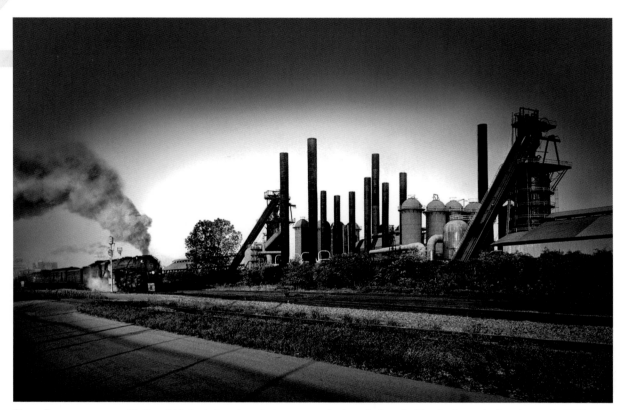

Sloss Furnaces, now a National Historic Landmark, began producing pig iron in Birmingham during the early 1880s. Norfolk and Western No. 1218 can be seen approaching on the main line from the west.

CHESAPEAKE & OHIO NO. 490, 1926

In 1926, the American Locomotive Company constructed No. 490 for the Chesapeake & Ohio Railway. It was built as a 4-6-2 Pacific-type locomotive for passenger service. The Chesapeake & Ohio was primarily a freight-hauling, mostly coal, railroad, but it wanted to attract more passenger traffic. In 1941, the railway ordered a set of eight new 4-6-4 Hudson-type steam locomotives from Baldwin Locomotive Works, and beginning in 1946, five of its existing 4-6-2 Pacific-type locomotives were rebuilt as 4-6-4 Hudson-type engines. No. 490 was one of the five. These Hudsons were larger than the more famous New York Central Hudson-type locomotives.

As a part of the rebuild, the cosmetics of the locomotives were also restyled to better compete with the streamlined, art deco designs of other railroads of the time. The five locomotives were shrouded with striking streamlining in classic Chessie yellow and stainless steel. Matching sets of streamlined passenger cars were also ordered. The intent was to use the locomotives on the railroad's most important passenger lines, including the Washington, D.C., to Cincinnati route. Because the transportation world changed so much after World War II, the streamlined Hudsons were never used for the glamorous service envisioned by Chesapeake & Ohio management.

Of the streamlined Chesapeake & Ohio Hudsons, only No. 490 remains today. It was stored in the railroad's Huntington Roundhouse until 1968, when it was moved to the Baltimore & Ohio Railroad Museum. Today, the locomotive can be seen indoors at the museum. It weighs almost 390,000 pounds and has 74-inch drivers.

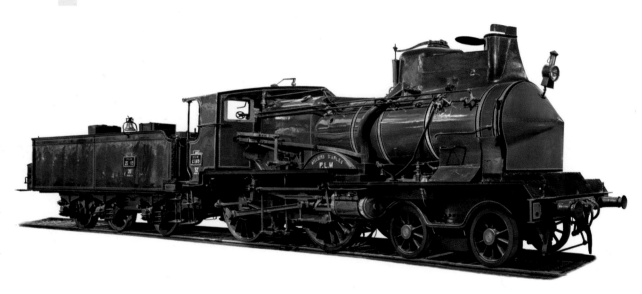

In an era several decades before streamlining became fashionable for railways such as Chesapeake & Ohio, the French introduced the Coupe Vent design in 1900. The unusual pointed cab and casing between the chimney and the dome was an early attempt to make large engines more aerodynamic as they "cut through the wind."

New York, Chicago & St. Louis No. 170, 1927

In 1927, the New York, Chicago & St. Louis (Nickel Plate Road) received its first order of 4-6-4 Hudson-type locomotives from the American Locomotive Company (Brooks Locomotive Works in Dunkirk, New York) for use primarily on its Chicago to Buffalo fast passenger line. The locomotives featured 71-inch drivers, were coal-fired, and were relatively lightweight at just under 320,000 pounds.

The Nickel Plate ordered a total of eight of these locomotives in the late 1920s, with four additional locomotives coming from Lima Locomotive Works. No. 170 was one of the initial locomotives from American Locomotive Company, and it is characterized by a distinctive low smokestack and features smoke deflecting wings, or lifters, to keep smoke out of the cab. This styling gives the locomotive a very fast appearance—even standing still.

Because these locomotives were best suited for express passenger operations and not freight or local passenger runs, they were early candidates for diesel-electric replacement and operated for a short 16 years. No. 170 is the only survivor of the scrap line. It can be seen in excellent cosmetic condition at the Museum of Transportation in St. Louis.

This colorful cutaway shows a steam engine valve and piston arrangement.

Atchison, Topeka & Santa Fe No. 3759, 1928

No. 3759 was the last steam locomotive to leave Los Angeles and travel through Cajon Pass, across the Mojave Desert, and on to Arizona, en route to eastern destinations. Between its delivery in 1928 and retirement in 1953, No. 3759 logged almost 2.6 million miles, primarily in passenger service along this and similar routes. This 4-8-4 Northern-type locomotive was built by Baldwin Locomotive Works with 73-inch drivers and was originally coal-fired.

In 1936, it was converted to oil, and as part of a rebuild, 80-inch drivers were installed. The engine was donated to Kingman, Arizona, in 1957 and placed on display in a scenic downtown park near Kingman Canyon.

The 4-8-4 Northern-type wheel arrangement largely replaced the Mikado and Hudson types on long runs for passenger and freight operations. The four leading wheels assured stability, and the four trailing wheels supported a sizable firebox. The eight drivers provided adequate traction, and the locomotive would still negotiate relatively tight turns. Longer and heavier trains were possible compared to earlier designs, and the generous tenders supported fewer water and fuel stops along the way.

The Santa Fe put its Northerns to work on trips between Chicago and Los Angeles. They proved to be very reliable and provided decades of service. The 4-8-4 wheel arrangement was used by all three of the big American steam locomotive builders and by several large railroads that built their own locomotives.

Historic brass plates for each of the Big Three American steam locomotive builders

Hammond Lumber Company No. 17, 1929

Many locomotives were built for and used in logging and timber operations across the Pacific Northwest. Hammond Lumber Company No. 17 is an example of a large 2-8-2T tank-type locomotive built by the American Locomotive Company in 1929 for logging operations. The locomotive was built for the Crossett Western Company in Oregon. Because much of the company's timber holdings burned in a major fire at about the time the locomotive was delivered, it was used during the 1930s and early 1940s as part of an extensive salvaging operation.

In 1942, it was sold by Crossett to Hammond Lumber Company in California. A few years later, the locomotive was stranded at a logging camp when fire destroyed access trestles. No. 17 sat idle in the woods for a number of years because the cost for rebuilding the trestles was more than the locomotive and the timber in the area were worth. In 1956, Georgia Pacific Corporation acquired Hammond Lumber and sold the 85-ton locomotive, which was subsequently disassembled and trucked out of the forest. It was reassembled, and in the mid-1960s, it began tourist operation on the Klamath & Hopow Valley Railroad.

Following the energy crisis of the 1970s, the tourist railroad went out of business, and No. 17 ultimately came to Mount Rainier Scenic Railroad, where it was restored and began operation in 1995. Today, No. 17 is in beautiful cosmetic and operational condition, and it pulls excursions between Elbe and Mineral, Washington, just below Mount Rainier.

Hammond Lumber Company No. 17 pulls into Mineral, Washington.

TRANSITION FROM STEAM TO ELECTRIC AND DIESEL

Through the Golden Era and as late as the 1930s, steam remained the dominant tractive technology for mainline passenger and freight operations across America, although electric and then diesel alternatives were under intense development. Steam engines from this era were powerful, and their infrastructure and operations were firmly established.

In 1895, General Electric completed the first mainline electric railway in the United States through the Howard Street Tunnel in Baltimore. As the 20th century began, electric designs were applied to trolleys, elevated rail lines, mining operations, and other special applications where smoke, sparks, and steam were a problem or a danger and where electricity was readily available. By 1920, electric locomotives had proven their mainline prowess, were clean in operation, and were low in maintenance costs. However, electrical systems were prohibitively expensive for most routes across the great expanses of the United States and Canada, as wires had to be strung over literally every foot of track, including railyards.

The key in the transition from steam to electrical systems came when a diesel engine and generator were added onboard an electric locomotive. Diesel-electric locomotives were fast, reliable, flexible, and cheap to operate. Although initial costs were higher than for steam, their manufacture could be standardized, they could be mass-produced, and less infrastructure was required. The transition came first to switching operations and later to the main lines. With each design advancement, the diesel-electrics became more and more powerful and more able to compete with steam. The full transition from steam to diesel-electric traction was delayed by World War II but was essentially complete by 1960.

Montreal Park & Island Railway / Cornwall Street Railway No. 7, 1901

Montreal Park & Island Railway/Cornwall Street Railway No. 7 is the oldest surviving electric locomotive in Canada and one of the oldest in the world. It was built by Montreal Street Railway in 1901 (some accounts indicate 1899) as engine No. 1 for the Shawinigan Falls Terminal Railway. The railway provided essential service to the Shawinigan Water & Power Company (now part of Hydro-Quebec) in the construction of a series of six dams on the Saint-Maurice River just east of Montreal, Quebec.

The locomotive operated on 50-horsepower motors with 600-volt direct current from the original Shawinigan Power station. In 1903, it was used to pull a train carrying the Governor-General of Canada, Lord Minto, on a visit to see the Shawinigan hydro and industrial facilities. In 1907, much of the Shawinigan operations, including the railway, converted to alternating current and the locomotive was removed from service. In 1912, it was sold to Niagara, St. Catharines & Toronto Railway, where it was rebuilt and went to work on the Niagara Falls Peninsular in Ontario. From 1931 until 1946, the locomotive was operated by Cornwall Street Railway as No. 7 and pulled freight cars for connections with the Grand Trunk Railway. Finally, in 1946, it was transferred or loaned to the Courtaulds Company, where it worked until having an accident in 1958.

Remarkably, the historic little locomotive was saved from salvage by the Canadian Railroad Historical Association in 1959, and between 1997 and 2001, it was restored to its 1946 appearance. Today, the locomotive is on display in the main hall of Exporail, along with a vast collection of historic Canadian locomotives and rolling stock.

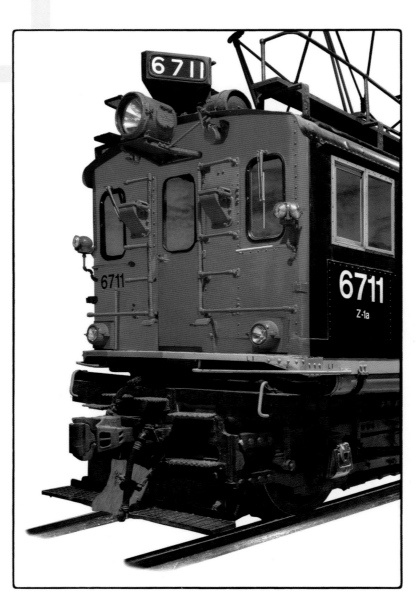

Canadian National Railway No. 6711, 1914

This General Electric locomotive, along with five similar locomotives, provided suburban and freight electric rail services in the Montreal, Quebec, area. It is now at Exporail, Saint Constant, Quebec.

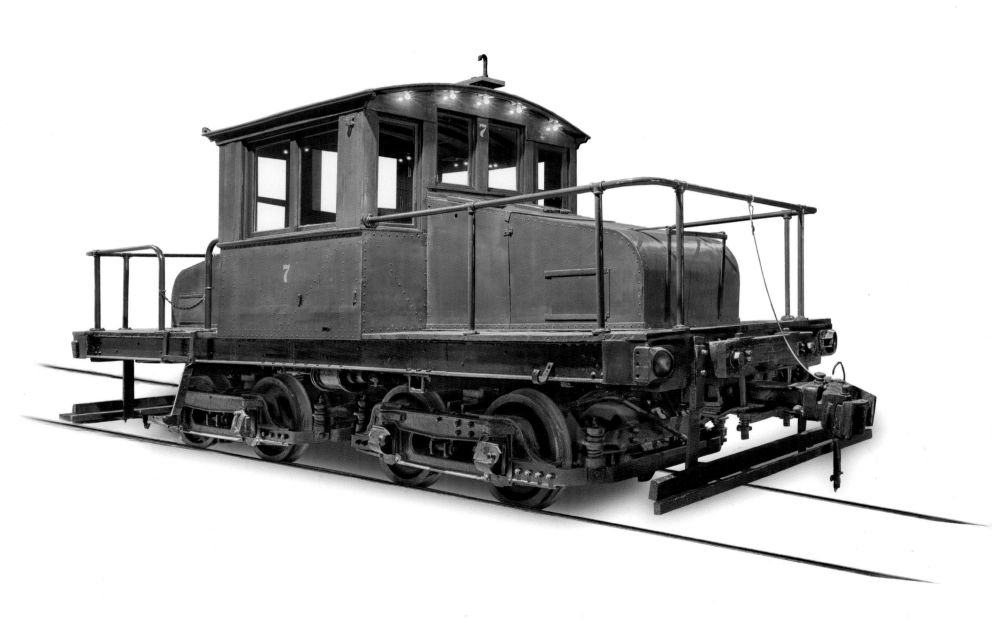

Niagara Falls Ice Drag, ca 1902

In 1895, Nikola Tesla and George Westinghouse completed the Adams Power Station, the first of several power stations at Niagara Falls. The Niagara Falls Adams Power Station was the largest in the world at that time. Winters were, and still are, frigid at Niagara Falls, and the river would ice over and reduce and limit power production. Removing the ice with hand tools was a dangerous and laborious job.

To help keep the station intake free of ice, a small electric locomotive, known as the Niagara Falls Ice Drag, was devised to break up and remove ice before it could enter the forebay area and clog the intake racks at the powerhouse. For many years, the Ice Drag moved back and forth in the winter to ensure that water flow was not reduced or obstructed by ice. This was a very significant early demonstration of an electric locomotive in an industrial setting. Today, the locomotive is displayed adjacent to a stone walkway near Horseshoe Falls on the Canadian side of the river. The locomotive weighs about 35,000 pounds and is equipped with drag rakes that can extend down into the water from an adjacent track.

Within just a few years after Adams Power Station began operation, alternating current would be applied for electric locomotive operation in many areas across the world. Alternating current could be transmitted over long distances and the voltages could be adjusted for both optimal line transmission and for ultimate customer use. Direct current on the other hand, required that power generating stations be built all along the rail line, maybe one every mile or so.

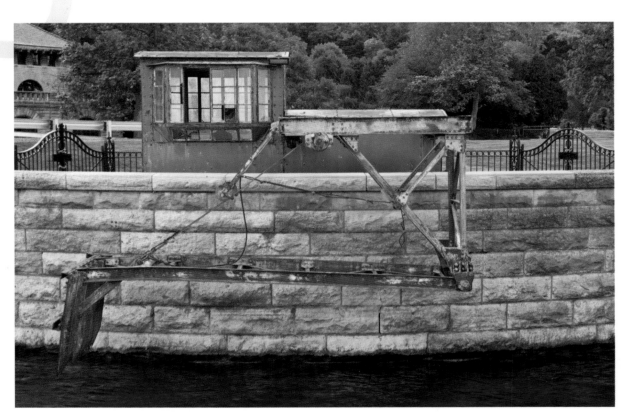

Niagara Falls Ice Drag with rake above the canal at Niagara Falls

ELECTRA, 1902
PACIFIC ELECTRIC NO. 1544

In 1902, this early electric locomotive was built in the North Shore Railroad Shops (formerly North Pacific Coast Railroad) for use north of and in the San Francisco area. It was based on four early General Electric traction motors. The locomotive was designed for overhead electrical service through a pantograph mechanism, and it ran on standard gauge track. The sloped front and rear sections, or ends, of the locomotive were actually taken from steam locomotive tenders. The design is sometimes referred to as a "steeple cab" to describe a design with a high cab near the center of the locomotive with equipment below.

The locomotive was affectionately known as *Electra* at the North Shore and that name carried over through succeeding ownership at Northwestern Pacific and Pacific Electric. This historic locomotive is best known for providing vital cleanup services after the 1906 San Francisco earthquake. Interestingly, in an era when the electrical grid was still developing, *Electra* drew so much power when it operated that streetcars and any other equipment on the same line could barely move. As a result, it was often used at night and in other off-peak periods.

When *Electra* was transferred to Pacific Electric in 1917, it was added to the roster as No. 1544. With Pacific Electric, *Electra* traveled south and was employed in subway tunnel construction under Los Angeles, where its clean electric technology was welcomed underground as an alternative to steam and smoke. It retired as a switch engine from the Pacific Electric Torrence Shops in 1952. After retirement, *Electra* moved to Griffith Park's Travel Town in Los Angeles, where it is displayed in distinctive Pacific Electric red coloring.

Electric locomotive technology evolved rapidly during the early years of the 20th century. One of the most interesting developments was the battery-powered industrial locomotive. North Staffordshire Railway No. 1, 1917, along with a few other battery-powered locomotives, were operating a century ago in industrial settings, especially at sites with the potential for fire or explosion. It is on display at the National Railway Museum, York, United Kingdom.

TUNNEL RAT / S-MOTOR NO. 113, 1906
NEW YORK CENTRAL & HUDSON RIVER NO. 113

Historically, the New York Central S-Motors are recognized as among the most significant locomotive designs ever produced. Beginning in 1904, the doubleheader S-Motors became the first mainline electric locomotives to be produced in quantity. No. 113 and the other S-Motors were built as an early joint effort of the American Locomotive Company and General Electric Company in 1906. Electric locomotives of this design are known by admirers as "Tunnel Rats."

Some S-Motors continued service into the 1970s, first in commuter operations and then as switching engines. They operated on 660 volts of direct current using third-rail technology with four 550-horsepower (410-kW) traction motors and were capable of speeds up to 60 miles per hour. Third-rail electric supply was required because of low overhead clearance in the tunnels; the rails were insulated to protect workers from possible electrocution.

S-Motors were developed as a result of the tragic 1903 Park Avenue Tunnel accident that killed 15 and injured many more in a smoke-filled tunnel beneath the city. Steam locomotives were not allowed in New York City tunnels or anywhere in Manhattan after June 1908. This regulation eliminated safety and air pollution issues associated with visibility on the tracks, especially in tunnels.

No. 113 was donated to the Museum of Transportation in St. Louis by the New York Central Railroad in 1963. The locomotive is painted in New York Central dark gray, which is almost black in tone. A total of 47 S-1, S-2, and S-3 Tunnel Rats were produced between 1904 and 1909. Three remain today.

Salt Cellar E1, 1900

Following the success of electric locomotives in a tunnel below Baltimore, Maryland, in 1895, eight steeple-cab locomotives with electrical systems from General Electric were ordered for operation below Paris.

PENNSYLVANIA RAILROAD NO. 3936 AND NO. 3937, 1910–1911

(DD-1 LOCOMOTIVES)

In 1910 and 1911, the Pennsylvania Railroad introduced the Class DD-1 electric locomotive series for operation in the New York City area, where regulations prohibited steam locomotives after June 1908. These smokeless locomotives accessed Manhattan through tunnels under both the Hudson and East Rivers.

The DD-1s were huge, fascinating machines and looked something like a hybrid of an electric locomotive of the era mounted on a steam locomotive drive chassis with a 4-4-0 wheel arrangement. They weighed more than 300,000 pounds and were powered by 2,000-horsepower (1,500 kW) Westinghouse direct-current motors. They were very quiet in operation and proved to be highly reliable.

Thirty-three pairs were built at the railroad's Altoona Shops by the Pennsylvania Railroad and Baldwin Locomotive Works. They drew power from a third rail and were capable of speeds to 85 miles per hour with their massive 72-inch drivers and side rods. A DD–1 locomotive set consisted of essentially two 4-4-0 units coupled back-to-back, and they were never operated separately.

Nos. 3936 and 3937 are the only remaining examples of this technology, and they are preserved at the Railroad Museum of Pennsylvania in Strasburg.

During the early 20th century, European railways followed the American lead in electrification. The locomotive in the right foreground is a ca 1915 design built by Westinghouse. In Europe, electrification was investigated because coal was scarce and costly in many regions, electric locomotives provided good traction on mountainous terrain, and hydroelectric energy was often available.

MILWAUKEE ROAD NO. E-2, 1919–1920

(BIPOLAR LOCOMOTIVE)

As World War I came to an end, the Milwaukee Road ordered a set of five very large, powerful, and distinctive electric locomotives to be built jointly by General Electric and American Locomotive Company. These massive machines were delivered in 1919 and 1920 and were commonly known as bipolars because they used bipolar electric motors to assure simple and reliable operation. The bipolars could pull trains that had previously required double-headed steam, and they were almost maintenance-free in operation for over three decades.

As is obvious from photographs, these exotic locomotives were striking and unique in appearance, and they came to represent the railroad in advertisements and promotions well into the 1950s. The public loved the way they looked.

In terms of design, bipolars weighed more than 520,000 pounds, and they were powered by 12 bipolar motors attached directly to the locomotive drivers. The motors received power through two overhead pantographs for a top speed of 70 miles per hour. The locomotives were about 76 feet in length and consisted of three separate sections permanently connected by ball-and-socket joints. The center section was the operations cab, and it included a steam generator for passenger heat. The end sections contained all the electrical components.

Unfortunately, the bipolars were poorly rebuilt in 1953, and all were retired by the end of the decade. Only No. E-2 remains today, and it can be examined at the Museum of Transportation in St. Louis.

This perspective view of Milwaukee Road bipolar E-2 shows the design of the rounded nose. The locomotive looks more angular from the side.

INGERSOLL-RAND NO. 90, 1926

(BOXCAB)

No discussion of historic locomotives would be complete without introducing the first commercially successful diesel-electric locomotive, known at the time as an oil-electric and called a boxcab. Diesel technology began developing in the late 1800s, but the early designs were very bulky and heavy, requiring extensive auxiliary systems for compression, cooling, and other functions. As was the case with early steam engines, these early diesel engines were large, stationary, and rambling contraptions and not very powerful. Because steam locomotives were so established and accepted at the turn of the 20th century, the incentive to develop a diesel locomotive was marginal at best, but work moved along over a period of several decades leading up to the introduction of this history-changing locomotive in 1926.

No. 90 was built through a partnership between American Locomotive Company (running gear and chassis), General Electric (generator and electrical system), and Ingersoll-Rand (diesel engine). This partnership was sometimes known by the acronym AGEIR, formed from the names of the principals. No. 90 was powered by a 300-horsepower (220 kW) engine. This basic model was a 60-ton locomotive; a 100-ton version was subsequently equipped with two of the same power systems.

No. 90 was used as a switch engine at the Ingersoll-Rand plant in Phillipsburg, New Jersey. Through this role at the plant, the locomotive also served as a demonstrator for sales and marketing. Of special note, No. 90 was the first locomotive to use roller bearing trucks. In 1970, it was donated to the Henry Ford Museum, in Dearborn, Michigan, where it was cosmetically restored for exhibit. A few other boxcabs can be discovered in museum exhibits around the United States and Canada.

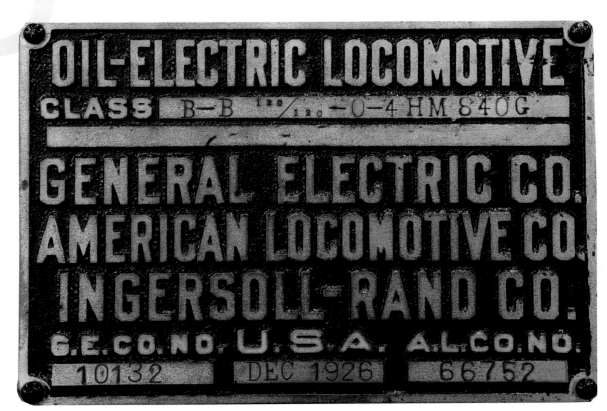

The brass plaque from boxcab No. 90

CORNWALL ELECTRIC RAILWAY NO. 17, 1930

(STEEPLE-CAB LOCOMOTIVE)

In 1895, Baldwin Locomotive Works and Westinghouse Electric Company formed a partnership to develop alternating current electric locomotives. (During this era, General Electric technology was direct current, and Westinghouse also offered direct current along with alternating current equipment.) Westinghouse actually completed a small boxcab locomotive in 1895 for experimentation, and by 1905, the partnership began marketing locomotives to several railroads, most notably the New York, New Haven & Hartford. Between about 1910 and 1930, steeple-cab-type locomotives were sold to railroads across the United States and in Canada. Very similar steeple-cab designs, such as the Trenitalia No. E626 005, were being built and tested across western Europe during the same time period.

No. 17 was built for the Salt Lake & Utah Railway in the United States as a 70-ton steeple-cab alternating current electric locomotive with four 200-horsepower motors. In 1954, it was rebuilt as an 80-ton locomotive and sold to Grand River Railway in Preston, Ontario. In 1963, it began operation for the Cornwall Street Railway Light and Power Company in Cornwall, Ontario, to handle freight between local industries and the Grand Trunk Railway. That railway became part of Canadian National Railway in 1971, and electric locomotive operations were ended.

No. 17 was restored in 1981, and as of 2017, it is on prominent exhibit with a historic marker in a park area of Cornwall.

Trenitalia No. E626 005, 1928, was one of the first group of steeple-cab electric locomotives designed and built in Italy. Like the Milwaukee Road bipolars and No. 17, these were massive machines that replaced steam locomotives. A total of 448 units were produced, and some actually remained in service into the 1980s, with several still used to pull historic tourist trains.

GALLOPING GOOSE, 1933
RIO GRANDE SOUTHERN NO. 5

By the time of the Great Depression, the operation of steam locomotives for much of the year and on most days of the week could no longer be justified economically across western Colorado. In 1933, the Rio Grande Southern Railroad was in poor financial condition and came to an appointed receiver, who concocted a scheme to keep the railroad running. The idea was to introduce economical railcars to the line. These were not to be the stylish European designs of Bugatti or Fiat, but homemade vehicles assembled from old automobiles, buses, and boxcars.

These crude railcars could serve a few passengers, carry a little freight, and most importantly, transport U.S. mail. The Rio Grande Southern called their design a "motor," but the observing public preferred the name *Galloping Goose* because they appeared to waddle down the tracks. The goose scheme returned the railroad to profitability. It was not until a few years after World War II, when the mail contracts were lost, that the railroad was set back. Still determined to survive, a few more seats were added to the cargo area of several geese, and tourist service took over where mail and freight had been carried. Operations continued into the early 1950s.

Of the seven original geese railcars, six remain and all are now operable. *Galloping Goose No. 5* was fabricated from a 1928 Pierce-Arrow limousine body and drive train, and was later rebuilt with a surplus gasoline truck engine and a Wayne school bus body. This amazing machine ran until 1952, the last few seasons with seating for 20 tourists. In 1997, No. 5 was restored by the Galloping Goose Historical Society of Dolores. It now makes popular excursion runs on the Cumbres & Toltec Scenic Railroad and the Durango & Silverton Narrow Gauge Railroad.

J. G. Brill / Mack Railbus No. 21, 1921

Rio Grande Southern was not the only railroad to operate railcars and railbuses. Railbuses operated on other low-usage lines. This classic, old gasoline railbus was operated by the Lewisburg, Milton & Watsontown Railroad, Pennsylvania Railroad, and Strasburg Rail Road. It is now at the Railroad Museum of Pennsylvania.

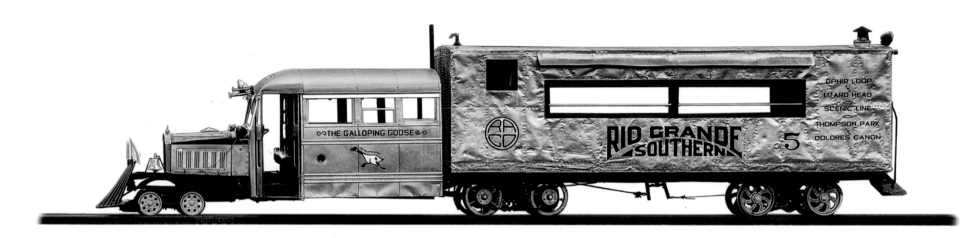

PENNSYLVANIA RAILROAD NO. 5690, 1934

Pennsylvania Railroad No. 5690 is a beautiful and rare early American electric switch engine. It was built in 1934 at Pennsylvania Railroad's expansive Altoona Works. The 570-horsepower machine was designed to receive power through a roof-mounted pantograph from an 11,000-volt overhead alternating current line.

The locomotive was used to switch passenger cars around the railroad's electrified yards and stations, primarily in New York City, Philadelphia, and Harrisburg, while reducing smoke in tunnels and around nearby stations.

The chunky little engine has a boxcab design, and it weighs about 157,000 pounds. To the Pennsylvania Railroad, this was a Class B1 switching locomotive.

Pennsylvania Railroad was one of the few electrified railroads in the United States, especially during this era. Its electrified system forms an important part of what is today referred to as the Northeast Corridor, which is used by Amtrak and commuter lines.

No. 5690 is preserved at the Railroad Museum of Pennsylvania in outstanding display condition.

Most electric railways are powered by high-voltage overhead transmission lines. Electricity is transmitted from the lines to a locomotive through a mechanism known as a pantograph. The pantograph is a spring-loaded frame device on the roof of the locomotive. It is designed to maintain contact with overhead electrical lines through a lubricating graphite block and transmit the power to the motor(s) in the locomotive.

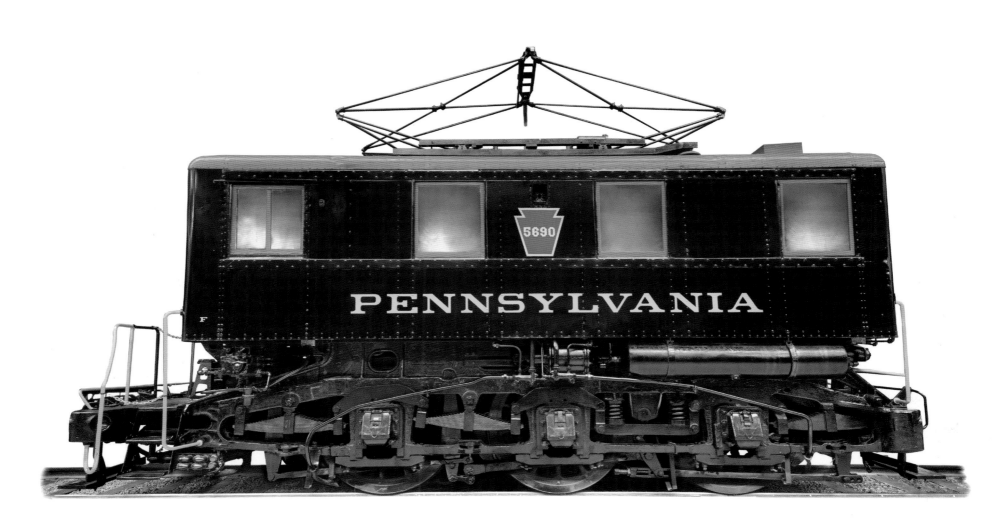

BIRMINGHAM SOUTHERN NO. 82, 1937

(HIGH-HOOD LOCOMOTIVE)

This attractive green locomotive with white trim and a red logo was built by the American Locomotive Company at Schenectady Works in 1937 as part of an order for five HH900 (HH stands for "high hood") units purchased by Birmingham Southern Railroad; three additional HH locomotives were subsequently purchased to replace steam equipment. No. 82 is powered by a 900-horsepower turbocharged diesel engine to produce 671 kW of electrical energy. The HH900s were the company's first turbocharged diesel locomotives and the first to exhibit the now-famous (and wildly popular with railfans) turbo-lag with a characteristic puff of black smoke as the turbine spins up.

No. 82 was sold to American Cast Iron Pipe Company in 1963 and ultimately became the second-oldest operating diesel-electric locomotive in the United States before retirement. It was donated to the Heart of Dixie Railroad Museum in Alabama, where it has undergone complete cosmetic restoration as of 2014.

American Locomotive Company was the American leader in diesel-electric locomotive manufacturing through most of the 1930s and into World War II. Of the Big Three steam locomotive producers, Alco became the most invested in diesel-electric technology. It continued to produce a successful lineup of diesel-electrics, especially switchers, road switcher (RS) locomotives, the FA/FB and PA/PB cab units, and the Century series road switchers through the 1950s and 1960s before finally falling victim to competition from General Motors and General Electric.

Reading Company No. 467, 1953

Beginning in 1941, Alco followed the HH models with a successful series of road switcher locomotives, including the RS-1 through the RS-3. Number 467 is a 1,600-horsepower RS-3 locomotive, which is now part of the collection at Steamtown in Scranton, Pennsylvania.

General Pershing Zephyr (Silver Charger), 1939
Chicago, Burlington & Quincy No. 9908

This sleek locomotive, also known as the *Silver Charger*, after World War I General John Pershing's horse, was built in 1939 and was the last of the streamlined, stainless steel Budd Company *Zephyrs*. The *Zephyr* concept and design was developed by Chicago, Burlington & Quincy, Budd Company, and Winton Engine Company. In 1932, Budd Company had demonstrated lightweight stainless steel railcar construction as a corrosion-resistant alternative to other metals and wood, and this concept was applied to the *Zephyrs*. The huge headlight was added as a safety feature because people in the 1930s were accustomed to noise, steam, and smoke as warnings of an approaching locomotive.

This *Zephyr* was powered by a 1,000-horsepower, V-12 diesel engine linked to an electric generator. The *General Pershing* was the only train in the *Zephyr* series that was not unitized and articulated in construction; the locomotive and each car was separate as with a conventional train and coupled for flexibility and customizing of train length. The *General Pershing Zephyr* was used extensively on a fast run between Kansas City and St. Louis and also served on many other routes during World War II. The locomotive continued in commercial service until 1966, while the rest of the stainless steel trainsets were retired soon after the war. Following retirement, No. 9908 was donated to the Museum of Transportation in St. Louis, where it remains on display today.

The first Burlington Route *Zephyr* began operation in 1934 and became known as the *Pioneer Zephyr*. The *Zephyr* concept was an immediate success in an era of declining passenger traffic and the Great Depression. The smooth and shiny streamlined stainless steel appearance and the blazingly fast service sounded a positive tone for the railroading industry and American society at a time when optimism was so desperately needed.

Sleek and streamlined, Chicago, Burlington & Quincy's *Nebraska Zephyr* operated between Chicago and Omaha and Lincoln, Nebraska.

CANADIAN PACIFIC INSPECTION CAR M235, 1939

This beautiful, rich blue Buick Special limousine was added to the Canadian Pacific Railway fleet in 1939 as a replacement for an older 1929 Packard. The M235 was fitted with air brakes, a truck's rear end, and locomotive-style horns for rail line operation. It could reach a speed of 79 miles per hour. This type of vehicle was used by superintendents to check up on crews and examine progress along road projects. Crews often dreaded the approach of an inspection limousine and the discipline that might follow a superintendent's visit. Today, the car is on display at Exporail in Saint Constant, Quebec.

As automobile components evolved over the first few decades of the 20th century, certain aspects of the improved technology were adapted to the rails. Major tire companies recognized a lucrative new market if they could successfully demonstrate the application of rubber tires for passenger trains. In the 1930s, Michelin tire company and Budd Company (builder of the *Zephyr*), with Goodyear as a contractor, promoted a series of rubber-tired locomotives that offered a smoother ride and quick acceleration and stops. The design was tested by Reading Railroad, Pennsylvania Railroad, and Texas & Pacific Railway as well as by railways in France. For a time, the locomotives went into commercial operation as the Texas & Pacific *Silver Slipper* and on prestigious commuter lines around Paris. Ultimately, the rubber tires could not support the weight required to provide necessary locomotive power for passenger trains but continued to be used on some subway coaches.

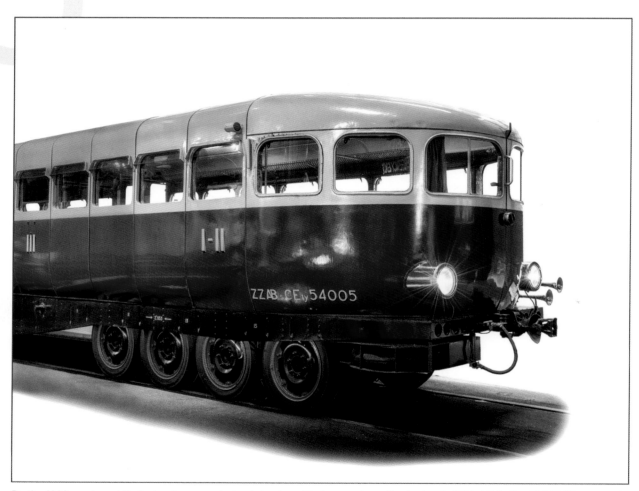

By the 1930s, automobile technology was being introduced to locomotives. Beginning in 1936, Micheline XM 5005 operated on 16 large tires to provide suburban rail service on select lines around Paris for those who would pay the premium. Tests in the United States by Michelin, Budd, and Goodyear were less successful.

EMC FT No. 103, 1939

Through the 1930s, diesel-electric technology evolved very quickly with several notable applications for both switching and passenger operations. During this decade, freight hauling remained the work of steam locomotives as General Motors strove tenaciously behind the scenes to develop a diesel-electric alternative. Then, in 1939, the Electro-Motive Corporation (soon to be the Electro-Motive Division of General Motors) introduced FT diesel-electric locomotives in an A and B set. (An A locomotive included an operator's cab while the B unit did not.) The No. 103 demonstrator was the first FT produced; it consisted of four separate 1,350-horsepower locomotive units assembled in an A-B-B-A set to achieve the power required for freight operations and compete with steam locomotives. A single crew could operate all four units.

The No. 103 locomotive set was referred to as a demonstrator because it was loaned around the country to various major railroads for evaluation. This set ran for 11 months in 35 states, on 20 different railroads, and for 84,000 miles with essentially no major problems. The set was efficient and economical and could haul freight as well as or better than competing steam locomotives. This demonstration proved to be a major factor in the rapid retirement of the steam locomotive fleet all across North America. In the six years after the demonstration, almost 1,100 FT locomotives were ordered. Every railroad that tried the No. 103 demonstrator placed an order.

No. 103A is now designated as a National Engineering Landmark and is preserved at the Museum of Transportation in St. Louis. Both the A and B units are painted in the original General Motors demonstrator dark green and gold; however, only the A unit is from the original A and B set.

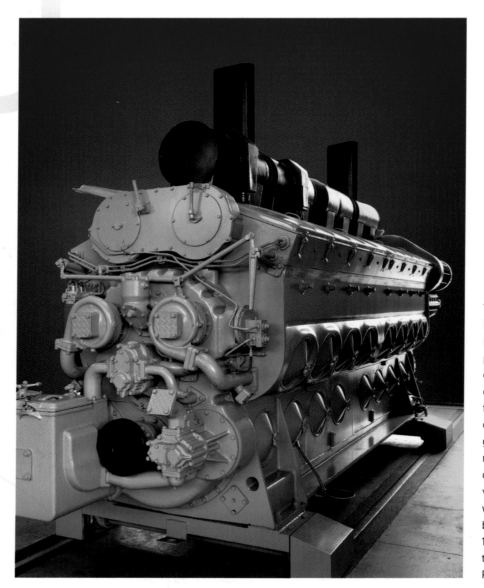

This view of an Electro-Motive Division 567 V16 prime-mover diesel engine is from the end of the engine that faces away from the cab. The main generator would be mounted at the opposite end. Several versions of this engine were produced between 1938 and 1966. (from Steamtown, Scranton, Pennsylvania)

PENNSYLVANIA RAILROAD NO. 4935, 1943

(GG-1 LOCOMOTIVE)

I n the early 1930s, during the depths of the Great Depression, the Pennsylvania Railroad undertook a massive design and construction project to electrify their operations along the main lines between New York City and Washington, D.C., in what would come to be known as the Northeast Corridor. The project involved new track, tunnel and bridge work, overhead electrical service, and other infrastructure upgrades. The project also called for a new high-speed electric passenger locomotive.

The result was the now famous, highly successful, and strikingly styled GG-1 series of locomotives. A total of 139 GG-1s were built between 1934 and 1943 by General Electric, the Pennsylvania Railroad's Altoona Shops, and several other key contributors. Famous designer Raymond Loewy added streamlined design elements. These locomotives were used exclusively in the Northeast Corridor, where overhead electrical service had been installed. At 79 feet, 6 inches and 475,000 pounds, GG-1 locomotives were huge, highly dependable, and capable of speeds to 100 miles per hour. Despite their length and weight, GG-1s were built with essentially a ball-and-socket at the middle and could flex to make tight turns and curves. Twelve 385-horsepower (4620 kW total) traction motors drove the GG1's 57-inch driving wheels on six axles. They were capable of peak operation approaching 8,000 horsepower, permitting rapid acceleration and effortless operation on steep grades. Most operated into the Amtrak era, with the last one retiring in 1983.

GG-1s were used to pull the funeral trains of both President Franklin Roosevelt and Robert Kennedy. The GG-1 has appeared in more movies and advertisements than any other locomotive design.

No. 4935 is preserved in excellent cosmetic condition at the Railroad Museum of Pennsylvania. This locomotive was built in 1943 at the Altoona Shops and was donated to the museum in 1983. The locomotive has been restored once and could be made operational again.

A GG-1 cab as viewed from the right-side entry door

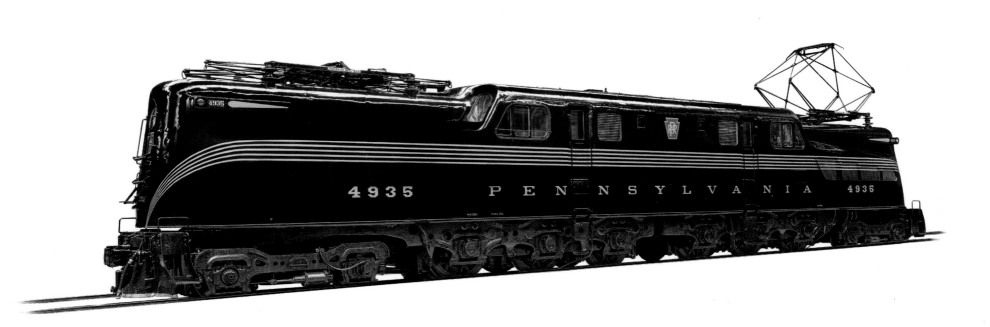